"From an investigative perspective, *Military Injustice* is a powerful, insightful must read for any military personnel and their families navigating the challenges and agony associated with military criminal charges. Mr. Callahan provides invaluable examples and expertise to help the reader comprehend the scope and realistic expectations of military criminal defense in straight forward, layman's language."

—Carolyn Martin,
Criminal Defense Investigator

MILITARY INJUSTICE

MILITARY INJUSTICE

PATRICK CALLAHAN

TATE PUBLISHING
AND ENTERPRISES, LLC

Published by Tate Publishing & Enterprises, LLC
127 E. Trade Center Terrace | Mustang, Oklahoma 73064 USA
1.888.361.9473 | www.tatepublishing.com

Tate Publishing is committed to excellence in the publishing industry. The company reflects the philosophy established by the founders, based on Psalm 68:11,
"The Lord gave the word and great was the company of those who published it."

Book design copyright © 2013 by Tate Publishing, LLC. All rights reserved.
Cover design by Samson Lim
Interior design by Jomel Pepito

Published in the United States of America

ISBN: 978-1-62510-667-4
1. Law / General
2. Law / Military
13.04.11

TABLE OF CONTENTS

COMMON ABBREVIATIONS IN MILITARY JUSTICE

AD sep:	administrative separation.
AFCCA:	Air Force Court of Criminal Appeals.
AUSA:	Assistant United States Attorney.
BCD:	bad-conduct discharge.
BOI:	board of inquiry.
CA:	convening authority.
CAAF:	Court of Appeals for the Armed Forces.
CDC:	chief defense counsel; *also* civilian defense counsel.
CG:	commanding general.
CID:	criminal investigation division.
CO:	commanding officer.
CRB:	competency review board.

DC:	defense counsel.
DD:	dishonorable discharge.
DI:	drill instructor.
DSJA:	deputy staff judge advocate.
GCM:	general court-martial.
GCMCA:	general court-martial convening authority.
IMC:	individual military counsel.
IO:	investigating officer.
IRO:	initial review officer.
LSSS:	legal services support section.
MCM:	*Manual for Courts-Martial.*
MJ:	military judge.
MJO:	*also* Mojo: military justice officer.
Mojo:	*see MJO.*
MOS:	military occupational specialty.
MP:	military police.
NMCCA:	Navy Marine Corps Court of Criminal Appeals.
NCIS:	Naval Criminal Investigative Service.
NC&PB:	Navy Clemency and Parole Board.
NJP:	nonjudicial punishment.
OIC:	officer in charge.
OQR:	officer qualification record.
OTH:	other-than-honorable (discharge).
PTA:	pretrial agreement.
PTC:	pretrial confinement.
RCM:	Rule for Courts-Martial.
RDC:	regional defense counsel.
RLS:	request for legal services.
ROT:	record of trial.

SAUSA:	Special Assistant United States Attorney.
SCM:	summary court marital.
SDC:	senior defense counsel.
SecDef:	Secretary of Defense.
SecNav:	Secretary of the Navy.
SJA:	staff judge advocate.
SJAR:	staff judge advocate's recommendation.
SPCM:	special court-martial.
SPCMCA:	special court-martial convening authority.
SRB:	service record book.
TC:	trial counsel.
UCMJ:	Uniform Code of Military Justice.
USA:	United States Army.
USAF:	United States Air Force.
USMC:	United States Marine Corps.
USN:	United States Navy.
XO:	executive officer.

PREFACE

This book has been many years in the making and countless hours in concept. It sparked as an observation and then quickly flamed into a grievance. From my early teens, I knew I wanted to serve my country's military. To me, one did not get more honorable than the ranks of the United States Marine Corps. When I joined as a starry-eyed teenager, this organization could do no wrong. But my experiences soon opened my eyes and changed my outlook. At first, I thought that it was simply a few isolated incidents or that it was just a few bad judge advocates and commanding officers that were causing injustices. However, the more cases I worked on, I came to understand that these injustices were not isolated incidents but mainstream problems. And while I fought for change, I made very little headway and almost no difference.

I quickly realized that simply having good judge advocates battle the system on a case by case basis was never going to establish change in what is an intrinsically flawed system. So I began pondering the problems and possible solutions. One problem that became apparent is that the public, and even most service members, are ignorant of the workings of the military justice system and its vast problems. I counseled numerous service members and families on these issues. I saw families who could not even begin to comprehend how their son, whose only goal in life was to be a Marine, could be branded a murderer by his own fellow Marines for combat actions in a war zone. I saw Marines who had dedicated their entire lives to the service of their country in the Corps who simply could not understand how that same Corps was determined to crush them the moment they were alleged to have committed a crime. I also saw serious offenders who were able to escape answering for their crimes because of flaws in how the military justice system operates. I determined that I could do more than fight injustices as they arose in specific cases—that I could educate the nation on the errors of the military criminal justice system and the terrible outcomes that it continually causes. And so was born *Military Injustice*.

This book specifically addresses the Marine Corps' criminal justice system. However, the majority of the problems are prevalent to varying degrees in the other services as well. The Uniform Code of Military Justice (UCMJ) is the primary source of law for all branches of the armed services. The Uniform Code of Military

Justice itself is the source of most of the unjust laws and procedures. So whereas this book addresses the Marine Corps' justice system specifically, the other branches are similar. The other branches use different terms and have varying nuances of law; however, this book aims to provide the reader with a solid understanding of the military justice system as a whole and its errors across all branches, not just the Marine Corps. The Navy's justice system is most similar to the Marine Corps, in part because they both fall under the Secretary of the Navy. Other than a difference in some of the terminology, the Navy's and Marine Corps' systems are virtually identical. The Air Force's justice system, although still very similar to the Marine Corps', is the most different. They, and to a lesser extent the Army, have taken steps to try to correct some of the injustices discussed in this book. Sadly, they both still have far to go as the most serious injustices stem from the source of law, the Uniform Code of Military Justice, that is universal across all the branches.

NOTE

The term *court-martial* is used in this book to refer to both general and special courts-martial unless the context indicates otherwise. It does not refer to a summary court-martial (SCM) unless specifically stated. General courts-martial (GCM) and special courts-martial (SPCM) are both criminal courts. A summary court-martial is an administrative punishment, not a criminal court.

THE MILITARY JUSTICE SYSTEM

KEY PERSONNEL

The military system of justice is entirely different from the American civilian justice system. It not only has different procedures, but it also has different personnel. To understand the military justice system, one must first understand its key personnel. The personnel of the military justice system can be divided into six categories: the command, the prosecution, the investigators, the defense, the court, and appellate. Each of these is discussed in detail.

The Command

Convening Authority

The command group is led by the most powerful person in the military justice system: the convening authority (CA). The convening authority is the military officer who controls the case. He is the commanding officer (CO) of the accused.* As the commanding officer, he decides whether or not to bring charges and what charges to bring. He is the one with the authority to enter into pretrial agreements (PTAs), or plea bargains as they are commonly referred to in the civilian justice system, on behalf of the military. These powers are most closely analogous to a district attorney (DA) in the civilian world. However, the convening authority, in addition to the powers of a district attorney, also has many other substantial powers. He picks the jury, or *members* as they are called in the military, that will hear the case. He also has the authority to grant or deny the production of witnesses and the expenditure of government funds by either party in furtherance of the case. Lastly, he also has the absolute discretion to grant any clemency that he feels is appropriate in a case.

> *The service member charged with a crime is referred to as the *accused* just as the civilian charged with a crime is called the *defendant*. Sometimes an accused will also be referred to as a defendant, but generally only by those more accustomed to working with the civilian criminal justice systems than the military criminal justice system.

The convening authority is not required to be an attorney, called a *judge advocate* or a JAG, and in fact very rarely is.* Only judge advocates serving in command billets** as a unit commanding officer can be a convening authority. Even in the Marine Corps, which is the most likely service to have judge advocates serving as commanding officers, there usually are not more than a couple judge advocates who are commanding officers at any given time.

*A judge advocate (JA) or judge advocate general (JAG) is a military attorney. They must have graduated from law school with a juris doctor (JD) degree and be admitted to practice law by a state bar association. All military attorneys are commonly called *JAGs*; however, that is not technically correct. The Navy has JAGs. In the Marine Corps, attorneys are judge advocates. This is because the Navy separates its officers by category. General war-fighting officers are referred to as *line officers*. Special support officers belong to other groups, called *corps*, such as the judge advocate general corps or the medical corps. In the Marine Corps, all officers are line officers (this is because every Marine is a rifleman). Since the Marine Corps does not split its attorneys off into a separate corps, they are not part of a judge advocate general corps and as such are not technically JAGs. Unless specifically stated otherwise, this book is referring to attorneys of all services when using the term judge advocate.

**A *billet* is a job position.

There are two types of convening authorities: those exercising special court-martial (SPCM) jurisdiction and those exercising general court-martial (GCM) jurisdiction.

Usually the battalion commander of a service member, or similar-level commander for units not broken down into battalions, will be the officer with special court-martial jurisdiction, called a *special court-martial convening authority* (SPCMCA). He will usually be a lieutenant colonel* or a colonel.**

*An O-5; a commander in the Navy.

**An O-6; a captain in the Navy.

Usually, the officer with general court-martial jurisdiction, called a *general court-martial convening authority* (GCMCA), will be the first general, or admiral, in a service member's chain of command. This officer is generally at least a brigadier general,* and he may be an even more senior general.

*An O-7; also called a *one-star general*. In the Navy, an O-7 is a rear admiral.

The convening authority's military justice duties are not his primary duties. As the commanding officer, his primary focus is accomplishing his unit's mission, and second to that is the discipline and morale of his unit.

Most bases have many convening authorities, but it depends on the size of the base. Large bases will often have a couple of general court-martial convening authorities and many special court-martial convening authorities. Typically, a small base will have one general court-martial convening authority and several special court-martial convening authorities, but some bases do not have a general court-martial convening authority at all, and they fall under the jurisdiction of a general court-martial convening authority located on another base.

Staff Judge Advocate

The convening authority has an attorney, called a *staff judge advocate* (SJA), who advises him on all legal matters involving his command, including military justice issues. Usually, a single staff judge advocate advises multiple convening authorities. A commanding general or admiral, who is a general court-martial convening authority, usually has his own staff judge advocate. In addition to advising the general court-martial convening authority, the staff judge advocate will also advise the special court-martial convening authorities who fall under the general court-martial convening authority's command.

The staff judge advocate is often responsible for overseeing the other attorneys that fall within the command, especially on smaller bases. The staff judge advocate is the senior officer and directly runs the law center in all Marine bases except Pendleton and Lejeune. Pendleton and Lejeune handle so many cases that they have what is called a *legal services support section* (LSSS). The legal services support section contains both the trial and defense counsel and is run by the officer in charge (OIC) of the legal services support section. The legal assistance offices on these bases are separate entities. The legal services support section handles all criminal matters; the legal assistance office helps service members, dependents, and retirees with various civil issues, such as family and consumer law matters. The defense counselors, although belonging to the officer in charge of the legal services support section, actually receive their fitness reports, or job evaluations, from the defense operational chain of command, which will be discussed later. However, the officer in charge of the legal services support section does have a fair amount of day-to-day administrative control over defense counselors and assigns them as either trial or defense counsel when they report for duty to the legal services support section. At Marine bases without a legal services support section, the staff judge advocate has the same functions as the officer in charge of the legal services support section in addition to his other duties. As such, the staff judge advocate oversees the trial counsel, review attorneys, legal assistance attorneys, civil law attorneys, and administratively controls the defense counsel. When judge advocates check into a base, the staff judge advocate assigns them their billet and reassigns them as he sees fit.

Some of the smaller bases, like Marine Corps Air Station Yuma (commonly referred to as *Yuma*), do not have a staff judge advocate. They have a director of the law center who fills essentially the same role as a staff judge advocate. A judge advocate is usually only called a *staff judge advocate* if he advises a general court-martial convening authority, and small bases like Yuma do not have a general court-martial convening authority at the base. This falls under a general court-martial convening authority located at another location, and he has a staff judge advocate that is located with him and advises him.

The deputy staff judge advocate (DSJA) assists the staff judge advocate in the performance of his duties and acts in the staff judge advocate's place when he is not available. The deputy staff judge advocate is usually the second most senior judge advocate at the command.

Adjutant / Legal Officer

The adjutant and legal officer are also part of the command. Although these are separate billets, generally the same officer holds them both.*

> *Usually the officer is an O-2 or O-3 for battalion-level commands. More senior commands, especially a division, usually have an O-4 in these billets.

The adjutant is the head personnel officer of a unit. The legal officer is responsible for the command's administration of any legal issues. He is not an attorney. The adjutant / legal officer duties include coordinating the issuing of administrative-type punishments, entering punishments in record books, and coordinating having members assigned, and assisting in ensuring witnesses from his command are present. Most adjutants / legal officers play a very small role in courts-martial. However, some adjutants / legal officers do have influence on the military justice system. This is more likely to occur at the battalion level for special court-martial convening authorities because the convening authority may rely on their advice on whether to send a case to a special court-martial or handle it administratively. However, most convening authorities rely on the staff judge advocate and the trial counsel for such advice if they are looking for it at all.

Sergeant Major and Executive Officer

Two other billets that are significant in the command structure but have little impact on the military justice system are the executive officer (or chief of staff for flag commands) and the sergeant major. The executive officer / chief of staff is the second in command of the unit. The sergeant major is the senior enlisted advisor in the command. Many junior service members, especially Marines, think that their sergeant major has a lot of influence in the military justice system and assume that he will look out for them. This often creates problems because Marines make incriminating statements to their sergeant major expecting to receive some leniency only to find that the sergeant major does not have the authority to grant any leniency, even if he wanted to.

The Prosecution

Trial Counsel

The main person in the prosecutorial team is the prosecutor, called the *trial counsel*. He represents the government in court. However, unlike prosecutors in the civilian justice system, he does not decide whether to charge someone, what to charge them with, or whether to enter into a pretrial agreement. He, along with the staff judge advocate, advises the convening authority on the cases that he is handling. Some convening authorities tend to follow the recommendations of their trial counsel. Some convening authorities tend to go only to their staff judge advocate for advice on criminal cases and some convening authorities pay little heed to either. The trial counsel also has the authority to issue subpoenas to obtain evidence that he feels is relevant to the case.* Most trial counsel are O-2s or O-3s, but they can be more senior. For example, the Marine Corps put together a special prosecutorial team to try war crimes cases from Iraq that included multiple trial counsel who were O-5s. Smaller bases may have only one trial counsel; a legal services support section will have around a half dozen.

> *A defense counsel does not have subpoena authority; they have to go through the trial counsel or the military judge in order to have a subpoena issued.

Military Justice Officer (MJO)

The head trial counsel is called the *military justice officer* (MJO). Depending on the size of the section he supervises, the military justice officer may try some cases himself or he may just monitor and train his section. He often assists with the difficult technical aspects of the cases his subordinates are prosecuting, and he handles the administrative tasks of leading his section. Because of their size, the legal services support sections actually have an officer in charge of the legal services support section in addition to the military justice officer. He is the senior officer at the legal services support section. The officer in charge of the legal services support section does not try cases and he handles administrative matters for both the trial and defense sections.

Staff Judge Advocate (SJA)

The staff judge advocate's involvement in actual cases depends largely on his personality and the size and number of the commands that he advises. Some staff judge advocates frequently get involved in the details of cases; some do not. For instance, during most of the years I was stationed at Marine Corps Recruit Depot–San Diego (MCRD San Diego)* the staff judge advocate was actively involved in just about every case the Depot had. There were not as many cases coming out of the Depot as most other bases because the Depot is much smaller, and as such, there were only two trial counsel and the military justice officers. When cases went to trial, especially some of the ones that had national media attention, the staff judge advocate would carefully supervise the trial counsel's handling of the case even down to minor details. Other staff judge advocates often limit their involvement to only major issues on major cases.

*Also called the *Depot*.

Clerks

The military justice section also has enlisted clerks who perform general tasks. Usually there are about the same number of clerks as there are trial counsel. The head clerk is called the *military justice chief*. The clerks handle administrative duties associated with the case for the trial counsel, such as coordinating witness arrivals and interviews, making copies, and generating various required forms. They are not paralegals, and like most enlisted Marines, most of them do not have college degrees.

Accuser

The last part of the prosecutorial team is the accuser. In the military justice system, someone, called an *accuser*, must swear an oath that the charges are true to the best of his knowledge. This is rarely someone with personal knowledge of the case. It is almost always one of military justice clerks. Other than swearing that the charges are true to the best of his knowledge and signing the charge sheet as such, the accuser has no role in the court-martial.

The Investigators

There are several different investigative agencies that handle military cases, and depending on the case, multiple different ones may be involved.

Command Investigator

If the command is the first to suspect an offense, or the offense is of a purely military nature, the commanding officer will often appoint a command investigator to look into the allegation. This investigation is often called a *JAGMAN investigation* because the Judge Advocate General's Manual contains the guidelines for conducting command investigations. The command investigator is generally an officer that is in the command who has no special legal or investigative training. The commanding officer can use the same officer for all investigations that arise, or he can appoint a different officer each time. Because a command investigation can be time consuming and is performed in addition to the officer's other duties, the commanding officer will frequently pick whatever officer is most able to handle the additional work. The command investigator will write a report, called the *command investigation*, and forward it to the commanding officer along with his recommendations for how to handle the case. Usually a command investigation is done for crimes of a military nature such as disobeying orders and disrespect or for minor offenses.

Criminal Investigative Division

The military police (MP) may also investigate the case. If this occurs, it will be handled by their Criminal Investigative Division (CID). CID agents are generally enlisted service members, who along with the other military police, answer to the provost martial. He is the senior officer in this section. However, the military is moving more and more toward civilianizing the police force and now includes civilian MPs and CID agents. CID agents are not required to have, and rarely do have, any college education. They go to the military occupational specialty (MOS) school—the military school that teaches one how to do their job—for military police, which is nine weeks long. After a few years of serving as military police, they are eligible to attend an addition school to become CID agents.

CID is entirely independent of the command and may investigate the case alone or in conjunction with the command. They may also investigate a case without the command's knowledge or even against the command's express wishes. However, they have no authority to send a case to a court-martial or to even administratively punish a service member. Thus, if the commanding officer is not interested in charging or administratively punishing the service member, CID will not usually spend time investigating the individual no matter what they believe he did or how strong they believe the evidence against him is. If the alleged crime is reported to the commanding officer, then CID will usually be involved. The commanding officer will often ask for CID's assistance in more difficult cases or in cases involving more serious crimes. CID is not required to do an investigation when the commanding officer asks them to. I served as defense counsel on several cases involving allegations of drill instructors assaulting recruits where CID was requested to investigate the case by the drill instructor's convening authority but CID refused to investigate the cases. This made things particularly difficult for the command and the trial counsel, since, in most cases involving allegations of drill instructor abuse, all the recruits under the drill instructor are potential witnesses and must be interviewed. In one of the cases, the command investigator had to interview several dozen witnesses and take written statements from them in addition to performing his other duties.

Naval Criminal Investigative Service

The Naval Criminal Investigative Service (NCIS) may also investigate the case alone or in addition to a command investigation and a CID investigation. NCIS agents are called *special agents* (SA), and generally they only investigate more serious crimes. They are not directly controlled by the military and are entirely independent of the command and of CID. Most NCIS agents are civilians, although some CID agents are sent to work as NCIS agents for a tour. NCIS agents attend about four months of formal training before being sent to their duty station. There they will be given an apprenticeship-type training by other agents and may eventually be sent to other formal schools for specialized training in a specific field of investigations. NCIS agents are also required to have a baccalaureate degree.

Like CID, NCIS may investigate a case without the command's knowledge or against its wishes, but they, too, lack the power to send anyone to a court-martial or to administratively punish them. NCIS frequently works with the trial counsel on the cases that they investigate after charges are preferred; however, they do not answer to the trial counsel. As such, sometimes they refuse to follow leads or look for evidence that the trial counsel wants them to. This forces the trial counsel to conduct his own investigation, which he may or may not be able to do depending on how much other work he has.

Civilian Law Enforcement

Civilian law enforcement may be involved in any criminal investigation as well. Sometimes they will coordinate an investigation with NCIS, but if they are involved, it is often entirely independent of both NCIS and the military. Civilian law enforcement is only involved if the case has off base criminal activity, which many do. As a general rule, the military can investigate what happens off base as long as the activity involves service members, but the civilian authorities cannot investigate or charge what happens on base. The military can prosecute a service member regardless of where the crime occurred, thus they will also investigate crimes occurring off base. Usually, civilian authorities, whether state of federal, lack jurisdiction over military personnel on military bases, and so they cannot investigate or prosecute what occurs on base. There are laws set up so that the United States Attorney's Office (USAO) can prosecute civilians in federal court for crimes that they commit on military instillations. The military, with a few very rare exceptions, cannot prosecute civilians, only service members may be court-martialed. Usually the military will have a trial counsel that assists the United States Attorney's Office in prosecuting the case. That trial counsel will also be a Special Assistant United States Attorney (SAUSA). On smaller cases, the Special Assistant United States Attorney may take the case into court on his own; on larger cases there will usually be a normal Assistant United States Attorney (AUSA) on the case as well.

Article 32 Investigating Officer

Lastly, in cases sent to a general court-martial, there will be a formal investigation, called an *article 32 hearing.** The convening authority must convene an article 32 hearing to send the case to a general court-martial unless the accused waives the hearing. However, at the conclusion of the hearing, the convening authority does not have to send the case to a general court-martial. He may still dispose of it at any forum he deems appropriate or he may take no action on the case.

*Because it comes from article 32 of the Uniform Code of Military Justice.

The article 32 hearing is presided over by an investigating officer (IO). The investigating officer is generally a judge advocate but is not required to be.* The investigating officer reviews the evidence—

testamentary, documentary, and physical—provided by the government and the defense. The investigating officer also has the authority to order additional evidence to be produced, although that is somewhat rare. He then makes a written recommendation to the convening authority on how to disposed of the case.

*In fact, in the Army, the investigating officer is usually not a judge advocate.

Article 32 hearings are often referred to as the military equivalent of a preliminary hearing; however, to compare them to a preliminary hearing is grossly inaccurate. The investigating officer can recommend that the charges be dropped and the convening authority can still send the case to a general court-martial. The government also does not have to present any evidence at the hearing, and the case can still go forward. Lastly, based on the recommendation of the investigating officer or on his own initiative, the convening authority can add more charges from the evidence presented at the article 32 hearing.

The Defense

Defense Counsel

The most important person in the defense category is the defense counsel. The defense counsel represents the accused. There are three different types of defense counsel: detailed defense counsel, individual military counsel, and civilian defense counsel.

When a service member is charged with a crime, he is appointed a detailed defense counsel to represent him. He can also request that a specific judge advocate represent him. If that request is granted, that judge advocate will serve as the accused's individual military counsel (IMC). He may serve as the sole defense counsel or along with the detailed counsel. Military defense counsel represents an individual free of charge. Additionally, an accused may also attain the services of a civilian defense counsel, but the government will not assist with the retention of that counsel or pay for their representation. Civilian counsel may also serve alone or along with any military counsel.

Defense Clerks

Defense counsel are provided defense clerks, who are attached to their section. The senior defense clerk is called the *defense chief*. Usually, there is only one defense clerk, so by default, he is the defense chief. He is usually a junior enlisted Marine whose role is strictly administrative support, such as setting up appointments and making copies. Occasionally, some of the more experienced and better educated defense clerks can be used to screen and locate witnesses as well.

Defense Investigators

An accused may hire a civilian private investigator to assist in his defense. Although a private investigator is an extra expense to the accused, depending on the case and the quality of investigator, they can be well worth the expense. The government investigators often only investigate with the goals of building a case for the government, so they do not pursue evidence that is favorable to the defense. Usually, defense counsel is either too busy or lacks the training and experience to engage in any meaningful investigation of a case so a private investigator can be a real asset to a defense team.

I have personally won cases that I probably would not have won had the accused not hired a defense investigator. In fact, in the very first case that I worked on with a defense investigator, one of the government's main witnesses testified differently from what he had told the defense investigator in an interview. After he testified, the defense investigator confronted him about his changed story, and he recanted. I recalled the witness, and once the military judge on the case heard him recant large parts of his testimony (it was a case tried by the military judge not a members panel), the government's case was sunk. The Military Judge acquitted the accused of all the more serious charges that he was facing. The accused was not sentenced to any time in confinement. Had that accused not hired the defense investigator, it is likely that he would have spent several years detained. Ever since then I have been a strong believer in defense investigators.

Senior Defense Counsel

The senior defense counsel (SDC) is the head defense counsel on an installation. He is responsible for training and supervising the defense counsel under him and for the administrative matters of his shop. He usually assigns defense counsel to their cases. Technically, the staff judge advocate, or officer in charge of the legal support services section, controls the detailing of defense counsel to cases, but as a general rule, he delegates that authority to the senior defense counsel. The senior defense counsel also serves as a defense counsel and represents clients.

Regional Defense Counsel

The senior defense counsel reports to the regional defense counsel. There are three regional defense counsel in the Marine Corps and they are lieutenant colonels. They oversee training and evaluations for their regions and offer court assistance on difficult cases. Most regional defense counsel do not take cases, although occasionally some regional defense counsel with substantial trial experience will take a few of the more serious cases. While I was the senior defense counsel at MCRD, San Diego the Marine Corps charged a couple dozen war crimes cases at Pendleton in a very short period of time. Many of these Marines were charged with murder. Due to the sheer number of cases, as well as how complex they were and what was at stake, the regional defense counsel ended up getting Marines from bases other than Pendleton, such as myself, to cover some of the cases, and he even personally represented some of the Marines.

Chief Defense Counsel

The three regional defense counsel answer to the chief defense counsel (CDC), who is the head defense judge advocate in the Marine Corps. His job is to make defense policies and to handle defense counsel ethical issues. He is also responsible for training and evaluations. He does not represent individual service members at courts-martial or otherwise. Although setting defense policy is important, his most important role is to protect the defense counsel under him from frivolous allegations of ethical misconduct. Several times I was wrongfully accused of unethical conduct when I was simply zealously representing my clients, and it always was of great comfort for me to know that the chief defense counsel was supporting me. This allowed me to focus on representing clients free of distraction and kept me from having any formal ethical complaints brought against me.

The Court

The Military Judge

The courtroom is run by the military judge (MJ). The military judge is a judge advocate between the ranks of major and colonel (O-4 to O-6.) He is in charge of the in-court proceedings even if the senior member outranks him.* His role is very much the same as that of a civilian judge, although he has significantly less authority (as discussed in the chapter "Military Judges Have Insufficient Power").

*It is not unusual to have a senior member that outranks the military judge in a general court-martial.

Members

In the military, the jury is referred to as the members' panel, or just as members. They are service members selected by the convening authority, and they decide the guilt or innocence and the punishment of an accused. However, the accused does not have to have a members trial. He may elect to be tried by the military judge alone. The convening authority must approve any finding of guilty that the members, or the military judge, reach, and he can always lessen any sentence adjudged by the members, or the military judge, but he cannot increase it.

Court Reporter

The court reporter records verbatim all that occurs in the courtroom. He is then responsible for taking that recording and transcribing it into the record of trial (ROT), which is a complete record of all that occurs in court for a particular court-martial. The court reporter also usually secures the evidence overnight during multiple-day trials, although the trial counsel may do that as well. Enlisted Marines serve as court reporters after attending the appropriate schooling. In the Navy, the trend has been to use civilians as court reporters, and the Marine Corps may eventually follow suit.

Bailiff

Although the military justice system does have a bailiff, his role is very limited. As a general rule, there is only a bailiff for trials with members, and he is simply a member of the convening authority's unit. The service member is assigned by the convening authority to be the bailiff for the trial without any special training. The bailiffs are not armed. Their responsibilities include calling "all rise" at the appropriate times and moving documents or items around the courtroom, such as taking papers from a counsel to the military judge or members. The bailiff's most important role is ensuring that the members are not disturbed or contacted while they are deliberating.

Security

For cases where the military judge deems it appropriate, security is provided for the courtroom. Some courtrooms have metal detectors and permanent security assigned, although most do not. For courtrooms without security, the military judge may request that Military Police be provided to act as security in particular cases where he deems it necessary.

Appellate

If the court finds the accused guilty, then the case proceeds to the convening authority's action. In the convening authority's action, the convening authority must approve the results of the court-martial.* If the convening authority approves any conviction, the service member may appeal the case. If the sentence approved by the convening authority includes a punitive discharge** or a year or more of confinement, the case is automatically appealed. A service member can also request an appeal on a case that is not automatically appealed. If the case is appealed, the accused will be assigned an appellate defense counsel who will review the record for errors. An appellate government counsel will also be assigned the case to represent the government. The first level of appeal is the service's court of criminal appeals.*** The final military appellate court is the Court of Appeals for the Armed Forces (CAAF). CAAF's rulings may be appealed to the United States Supreme Court. Cases can also be reviewed by federal district courts via a habeas corpus request; however, these are quite rare. One can appeal from the federal district court to the appropriate circuit court of appeals and then to the US Supreme Court as well.

*He can always lessen convictions and punishments, but he can never increase them.

**A dishonorable discharge (DD) or a bad-conduct discharge (BCD).

***The Navy and the Marine Corps share a court—the Navy-Marine Corps Court of Criminal Appeals.

SYNOPSIS OF A CASE

The primary law governing the Armed Forces is the Uniform Code of Military Justice (UCMJ). The Uniform Code of Military Justice is a federal criminal code that applies to the members of the Armed Forces. It is enacted the same way as the civilian federal criminal code. It is passed by both houses of Congress and signed by the president, or it is passed by Congress over the president's veto by a two-thirds majority. Laws passed by the federal government, including the Uniform Code of Military Justice, are codified in the United States Code (USC).

In addition to the Uniform Code of Military Justice, there are several other important sources of military law and regulations. The president, in his capacity as the commander in chief, often enacts executive orders dealing specifically with the military.

Regulations are also passed by the Secretary of Defense as well as the individual service secretaries (i.e., the Secretary of the Army) and the judge advocate general, often referred to as *JAG*, of the individual service. The Navy and the Marine Corps share a secretary (the Secretary of the Navy) and a judge advocate general. The service secretaries, like the Secretary of Defense, are civilians appointed to their posts by the president with the consent of the Senate. The service secretaries answer to the Secretary of Defense and the president. The judge advocate general of each individual service is the senior active duty judge advocate for that branch.*

> *The Marine Corps is an exception. In the Marine Corps, the senior judge advocate is the staff judge advocate to the commandant of the Marine Corps. Just as there is no secretary of the Marine Corps and the Marine Corps operates under the Secretary of the Navy, so

> the Marine Corps does not have its own judge
> advocate general and operates under the judge
> advocate general of the Navy.

The same as in the civilian world, most military cases are begun when someone makes an allegation of a criminal act. The allegation may be made to the military police or directly to the command. Who makes the allegation, the nature of the allegation, and whom the allegation is directed to determine the initial steps taken in the case.

When an allegation of a violation of the Uniform Code of Military Justice (UCMJ) is made to the command, the command must decide whether to treat the matter as a criminal matter or an administrative matter. The procedures for criminal matters, that is courts-martial, are discussed in this chapter. The procedures for administratively handling a matter, such as through nonjudicial punishment (NJP), are discussed in the next chapter.

The first thing that a commander does upon learning of an allegation is to decide whether it is appropriate to handle the allegation at his level or whether it should be forwarded to a senior commander for adjudication. For instance, if a platoon commander learns that one of his junior Marines is inexcusably late to work—technically a criminal violation of the Uniform Code of Military Justice—he will probably handle it at his level via an administrative action, either formally or informally, and the matter will be over. However, if that Marine committed a more serious crime, such as drug use or theft, the platoon commander should forward that matter to a higher authority for disposition.

The decision of whether or not to place a service member in pretrial confinement must also be made. Any service member serving in a law enforcement billet, any officer, or any noncommissioned officer may apprehend (the military term for *arrest*) a service member. Once a service member is apprehended, he must be turned over to a brig or to the military police for confinement. The service member with custody of the detainee* must notify the commanding officer of the detainee within twenty-four hours that the detainee is in custody and the offenses that he is alleged to have committed. Within seventy-two hours, the detainee's commanding officer must determine whether the circumstances merit pretrial confinement (PTC). If he determines that the circumstances do not justify pretrial confinement, then he must order the detainee released. If the commanding officer determines that pretrial confinement is warranted, he must so state in writing along with his reasons for the pretrial confinement. The detainee must then be brought before a neutral and detached officer, called a *magistrate*. The magistrate is not required to be a judge advocate. Magistrates are usually senior officers, O-5s or O-6s. The magistrate must hold a hearing to determine if pretrial confinement is warranted within seven days of the detainee's initial confinement. A detainee is entitled to representation by a defense counsel at the hearing; however, it is often not the counsel who will represent him at his court-martial, should the case proceed to a court-martial. The government is represented by a trial counsel and usually a command representative as well. The command representative is a senior member of the command present to reiterate the commanding officer's reasons for believing that the service member should stay confined.

> * Technically, a service member is not a prisoner until he is convicted.

To keep a service member in pretrial confinement, there must be probable cause, meaning that it is more likely than not, that a crime was committed, that the accused committed the crime, that confinement is necessary because either the service member will not appear in court or that he will commit other serious misconduct, and lastly that lesser forms of restraint, such as being restricted to the base, are inadequate.

If an accused is kept in pretrial confinement, he may, once his case has been referred to a court-martial, appeal the decision to keep him in pretrial confinement to the military judge assigned to his case. There is no bail in the military, which results in a significant number of individuals being held in the brig until their trial.

In all cases, whether or not pretrial confinement is imposed, a criminal case can only be brought by an officer with court-martial convening authority. The lowest level convening authorities are battalion commanders, the captain of a ship, or commander of a similar level unit. When a matter is brought to the attention of a convening authority, he must decide what type of investigation is appropriate for the case.

Normally, violent crimes or crimes involving large amounts of property damage are reported by the victim to law enforcement, either civilian or military. Law enforcement will then report the crime to the command. When crimes are first reported to law enforcement, Criminal Investigative Division (CID) or Naval Criminal Investigative Service (NCIS) will usually already have started an investigation on the case. Naval Criminal Investigative Service and Criminal Investigative Division are independent of each other and of the command. However, ordinarily, Naval Criminal Investigative Services and Criminal Investigative Division will not both investigate the same crime. Naval Criminal Investigative Service investigates the more serious cases, such as cases involving a death, kidnapping, rape, assault with serious bodily injury, arson, drug dealing, substantial property damage or theft, and so on. Criminal Investigative Division generally investigates less serious cases, such as assaults without serious injury, drug use, most thefts, and so on. If the convening authority feels that the case is appropriate for a Naval Criminal Investigative Service or Criminal Investigative Division investigation, he can request that they investigate the case; however, he cannot order them investigate it.* Likewise, he cannot keep them from investigating a case. However, the convening authority has the sole discretion whether to send a case to a court-martial; Naval Criminal Investigative Service or Criminal Investigative Division cannot send a Marine to a court-martial. During the course of the investigation, law enforcement provides written reports to the convening authority. These reports do not contain recommendations, just a summary of the evidence discovered and the action taken by law enforcement. Cases involving purely military offenses such as orders violations or disrespect are usually investigated by a command investigation, also called a *JAGMAN investigation* (because the judge advocate general's manual describes how to conduct such investigations).

> *The convening authority can order CID to investigate a case if he is their commanding officer.

When a command investigation is conducted, the convening authority appoints one of his officers as an investigating officer* and orders him to conduct the investigation. Most command investigations are done by a junior officer who is not particularly busy, but in cases where the convening authority believes that someone with more experience is required, he can appoint a senior office to conduct the investigation. The written investigation contains several sections: (1) a preliminary statement which describes the investigation; (2) findings of facts, that is, the facts that the investigating officer believes are relevant to the case (3) an opinions section where the investigator lists his opinions about the case, the evidence, and the witnesses; and (4) a recommendation, where the investigating officer makes his formal recommendations for handing the case to the convening authority. The investigation should also contain written statements from everyone the investigating officer interviewed.

*Not to be confused with an investigating officer who presides over an article 32 hearing.

Once the convening authority has the reports of the investigation, he must determine whether to pursue a criminal prosecution. He may also decide that the case merits no action or he may handle it administratively. A convening authority is not required to consult with his staff judge advocate prior to making such a decision. A convening authority may rely heavily on his staff judge advocate in determining whether to handle a case criminally or he may not consult with him at all; it depends on the relationship that each particular convening authority has with his staff judge advocate.

If the convening authority decides to pursue the case criminally, he will send a request for legal services (RLS) to the military justice office. The military justice officer (MJO, called the *Mojo*) will assign a trial counsel to read the investigations, make any additional inquiries necessary, and draft up charges. For more serious cases, the military justice officer may do this himself. Sometimes for minor military offenses, such as unauthorized absence, a senior clerk will draft the charges for a trial counsel to review them. The staff judge advocate may also review the charges and make any changes that he feels are appropriate, especially at smaller bases. Although it is not required before the charges are preferred, or formally brought against the accused, they will normally be sent back to the convening authority for approval. Technically, anyone can prefer charges but only the convening authority can decide whether to send preferred charges to a court-martial, a process called *referring*. Since only the convening authority can refer charges, trial counsel often ensure that the charges are as the convening authority wishes to refer them before preferring the charges. This is done to avoid having to re-prefer the charges if they are not as the convening authority wishes to refer them.

If the convening authority approves of the draft charges (if this step is used), the charges are then preferred. To prefer the charges, a person subject to the Uniform Code of Military Justice simply swears that they are true to the best of his knowledge and belief. A military justice clerk generally does this, although in actual practice they usually have not read the investigation and have no idea about the validity of the charges. Usually the trial counsel just tells the clerk that the charges are valid and the clerk swears to it. The individual who swears to the charges is called the *accuser*. Other than signing the charge sheet in the appropriate spot and thereby preferring the charges, he has no further role in the case. Once charges are preferred, a copy of them is given to the accused and they are sent to the convening authority for disposition. Once charges are preferred, an accused is entitled to a defense counsel. Although an accused is often aware that charges are pending and has even sought legal advice, a judge advocate is not officially assigned to his case until the preferral of charges. Of course, an accused may hire a civilian counsel at any time, even before preferral. Defense counsel are usually assigned to a case by the senior defense counsel. The power to detail a defense counsel cases actually belongs to staff judge advocate at smaller bases or to the officer in charge of the legal services support section at larger bases; however, the authority to detail cases is typically delegated to the senior defense counsel to avoid the appearance of impropriety. One major caveat is that the authority to co-detail defense counsel is not usually delegated. This can make it difficult to get co-counsel on more serious cases. Usually the individual military counsel (IMC) request is used if an additional military counsel is needed.

A service member has the right to choose a particular military attorney to represent him, provided that the attorney is reasonably available. This counsel is called an *individual military counsel*, or IMC. Judge advocates that are serving as trial counsel, government appellate counsel, military judges, instructors, students, staff judge advocate, or deputy staff judge advocate are never available per regulations. Thus, most individual military counsel are other defense counsel, although legal assistance attorneys or judge advocates serving in non-legal billets are sometimes approved as individual military counsel. Usually, a judge advocate is only going to be considered reasonably available if he is in same geographic location as the court-martial. The individual military counsel does not have to be in the same service as the accused.

A service member that wishes an individual military counsel must submit a request in writing for the judge advocate that they desire. The request is first sent to the convening authority. He reviews the request to determine whether the requested judge advocate is statutorily unavailable. If the judge advocate is statutorily unavailable, the convening authority denies the request. If the requested judge advocate is not statutorily unavailable, then the convening authority forwards the request to the commanding officer of the requested attorney. In the Marine Corps, defense counsel are supervised by other defense counsel, but their commanding officer is not a defense counsel. Defense counsel's commanding officer is normally the commanding officer of the headquarters and service battalion (H&S Bn) for the base where the defense counsel is located. It is of note that this officer is also a convening authority and will refer cases to trial against clients that the defense counsel is representing; however, this is addressed later in the chapter titled "Government Control of Defense Counsel."

Often the commanding officer delegates the authority to grant or deny individual military counsel requests to the staff judge advocate. Some staff judge advocates ask the defense counsel if he is available; some make the determination themselves. The controlling factor is usually the attorney's workload and the amount of time that will be necessary to serve as the individual military counsel. If the Marine belongs to a legal services support section, the officer in charge of the legal services support section may have the authority to respond to individual military counsel requests delegated to him instead of to the staff judge advocate.

Once the accused has been assigned a defense counsel, if the case is a special court-martial, the convening authority may immediately refer the case to a court-martial. If the case is tentatively a general court-martial, then it must be sent to an article 32 hearing, so named because the requirement for the hearing comes from article 32 of the Uniform Code of Military Justice, before it can be referred to a court-martial.

At an article 32 hearing, the charges and evidence are presented to an investigating officer (IO). The investigating officer is usually a judge advocate, although a junior one, but the investigating officer is not required to be a judge advocate.* The trial counsel may call witnesses. However, usually the individuals that investigated the case are the only witness called by the prosecution. The rules of evidence do not apply at an article 32 hearing so the investigations are usually presented as well. The defense also has an opportunity to present a case but frequently will not because they do not want to give the government a preview of their trial strategy. A good defense counsel will try to call all the government witnesses possible though. This allows him to cross-examine them under oath such that their answers can be used to impeach the witness at trial if he changes his testimony. It also allows the defense counsel to evaluate the witness and plan how to best deal with him at trial. Lastly, the investigating officer has the authority to call any witnesses or pursue any evidence that he wishes to as well, but this is also rare.

*In the Army, the investigating officer is rarely a judge advocate.

At the conclusion of the presentation of evidence, both sides will argue for what they consider an appropriate disposition for the case. The investigating officer only makes a recommendation for the disposition to the convening authority; the convening authority has the final authority to do as he wishes with the case. The investigating officer may recommend that the case go to a general court-martial, a special court-martial, be handled administratively, or be dropped. The article 32 hearing is often called the military equivalent of a preliminary hearing; however, it is nothing like a preliminary hearing since the investigating officer's determination is only a recommendation. I have had many cases where the investigating officer recommended that the charges be dismissed and yet my client still was sent to a general court-martial. One of the major problems with the military justice system is that the result of the article 32 hearing is not binding on the government; this issue is addressed in more detail in the chapter titled "Nonbinding Article 32 Hearings."

After the article 32 hearing, the investigating officer will make his written recommendation to the convening authority. His recommendation will be sent to the general court-martial convening authority, not the special court-martial convening authority.* The investigating officer's recommendation, called the *investigating officer's report*, or the *article 32 report*, is first routed through the staff judge advocate. The staff judge advocate will comment on the investigating officer's report and make his recommendation to the general court-martial convening authority as well. The staff judge advocate's recommendation is contained in the article 34 letter, so called because article 34 of the Uniform Code of Military Justice requires that the staff judge advocate to make a formal recommendation to the general court-martial convening authority as well. In practice, the article 34 letter is usually just a rubber stamp restatement of the investigating officer's report and often is not longer than a paragraph or two. Usually the staff judge advocate saves his more detailed thoughts and recommendations on a case for a face-to-face discussion with the convening authority since the article 34 letter is discoverable by the defense, but the contents of conversations between the convening authority and the staff judge advocate are rarely discoverable.

> * It is usually the special court-martial convening authority that actually convenes the article 32 hearing.

Once the general court-martial convening authority receives the preferred charges, the article 32 report and the article 34 letter, he makes a decision what to do with the case. He may take no action, direct that the case be handled administratively, send the case back down to the special court-martial convening authority for a special court-martial, or refer the case to a general court-martial.

Referral is the act of sending, or referring, a case to a specific court for trial. Referral is done the same way whether it is a general court-martial referral following an article 32 hearing or a special court-martial referral.

Each convening authority has a convening order which creates a court-martial. The convening order will list the service members which will serve as members, the military equivalent of a jury, for that court-martial. Usually each convening authority has a standing convening order which he then modifies to pick what members he wants for each specific case he refers to trial. The convening order can also have certain special instructions for the conducting of the court-martial, the most common one being an order to try the referred charges in conjunction with a pervious set of referred charges that has not yet gone to trial.

Once charges are referred, the trial counsel will send a copy of the charges to the military judge that is responsible for docketing cases along with a requested date to arraign the accused. Ideally, the trial counsel will consult with the defense counsel and request a mutually agreeable arraignment date, but that does not always happen. The defense counsel can submit a continuance request to the military judge asking to move the arraignment date if it is docketed for a date that the defense counsel is not available.

At the arraignment, the accused is formally informed of the charges against him. He also has the opportunity to select a forum and enter pleas. Forum selection is the election to be tried by a court composed of members or by the military judge alone. If the accused is an enlisted member, he may elect to be tried by a court composed of officer members or members with at least one-third enlisted representation. Generally speaking, an accused will defer forum selection and entering of pleas until after all the motions have been heard in the case. An accused is allowed to defer the forum selection because the outcome of the motions may determine the type of forum he elects. In actuality, an accused can almost always change forum as well any time before the trial begins. Pleas are deferred because by statute certain motions must be brought before entering of pleas and the motions are not heard until after the arraignment.

The arraignment is an important event for several reasons. First, it stops the speedy trial requirement. An accused must be brought to trial within 120 days of charges being preferred or pretrial confinement being imposed if he is not currently in pretrial confinement. If he is in pretrial confinement, the government must act with due diligence to bring the case to trial, which can be a much shorter period than 120 days. When an accused is arraigned, he is considered to have been brought to trial, even though the actual trial may not take place for many months after the arraignment.

Secondly, after the arraignment, the government cannot make any major changes to the charge sheet without the consent of the accused. A major change is a change that changes the time of the alleged offense, the place of the alleged offense, the actual crime charged, the alleged victim, and so on. Minor changes are to correct administrative errors, such as spelling errors. The government only needs to get the permission from the judge to make minor changes, and the judge will routinely grant such requests.

If the government wishes to make a major change after arraignment and the accused does not consent to the change, the government sometimes will elect to withdraw all the charges without prejudice and start over again with a new preferral. As a general rule, the government is able to do this; however, it is a major burden for the government, so it is usually only done if without the major change the government will be unable to convict the accused of the more serious crimes that he is charged with committing.*

*I have successfully argued before that the government could not dismiss without prejudice and recharge the case where they completely charged the wrong crime. In that case, a drill instructor was charged with punching one recruit and throwing something at another recruit, among other things. The government erroneously charged him with punching the one he allegedly threw something at and throwing something at the one he allegedly punched. Obviously, the government would be unable to prove the charges as they were. Unlike in the civilian justice system, in the military, the government is supposed to bring all known charges against an accused at one trial. I argued that the government was aware of the proper charges and simply failed to bring them and should be barred from later bringing them. The military judge agreed. The convening authority then chose to handle all the charges at an administrative forum. I have made that same argument on other cases as well; however, that is the only time it was successful. The majority of the time, the military judge is going to allow the government to withdraw the charges and reprefer them.

After the arraignment, the government also cannot add any new charges to the court-martial without the consent of the accused. Often an accused will consent to having the charges added to his current court-martial to avoid the possibility of facing two courts-martial. However, if the original charges are significantly more serious than the additional charges, the defense may refuse to allow the government to join the charges, hoping that the government will not go through the extra effort of conducting a second court-martial on the more minor offense.

> *As a general rule, the aggregate punishment from two courts-martial will be greater than the punishment from one court-martial for the same offenses.

The military judge will also set the trial milestones at the arraignment. The milestones are the dates that certain important events, such as witness requests and motion filing, must be accomplished by and the dates for the trial.

In order to avoid arraignments, a new trend has arisen called a *motion for docketing* (MFD). A motion for docketing is a motion filed by the counsel with the court requesting certain milestone dates agreed on by counsel. It also operates to stop the government's speedy trial requirement. An accused is then technically arraigned at the motions hearing date.

Motions for docketing are not found in the Uniform Code of Military Justice or in the *Manual for Courts-Martial*. They were created by a military judge as a way to save time. The government is often in a rush to arraign an accused since it stops the speedy trial clock. Many cases plead away after the arraignment. The motion for docketing was created in order to save the time required to conduct an arraignment in cases where it is not needed because the case will plead away to an administrative forum.

I have always steadfastly opposed the motion for docketing. It does not protect a client from major changes or additional charges. When the government charges someone, they are trying to take away his property and freedom. Defending that individual to the fullest extent of the law must come before ease and convenience. While on active duty, I fought with a great number of military judges over my refusal to enter into motions for docketing. They commonly tried to force me to agree to a motion for docketing by high-handed tactics such as ordering me to go trial in a very short time frame or by scheduling the trial over dates when I had leave; however, I still refused to enter into motions for docketing.

After the arraignment, or motion for docketing, the next major step is the witness request. The government has subpoena power and can order witnesses, civilian or military, to appear at a court-martial. The defense does not have subpoena power and must request the government to produce the witnesses that they want for the trial. Technically that request goes to the convening authority since he is the one that will have to pay for the production of the witnesses. However, in most routine cases the convening authority will allow the staff judge advocate or even the trial counsel to grant or deny witnesses on his behalf. If the government denies any defense witnesses, the defense may then file a motion with the court requesting that the military judge require the government to produce the witness. Technically the military judge cannot order the convening authority to produce the witnesses; all the military judge can do is order the case abated* or order that the case be dismissed. Military judges do not have injunctive power, that is the power to order people to do something or to refrain from doing something, like civilian judges do. The military judge will order that the witnesses be produced if they are necessary to the defense's case, that is if they are relevant and not unduly cumulative.

> *That is, order that the case be put in an inactive status and that no further court action will be taken on the case unless the convening authority does what the judge is wanting him to do.

The next milestone is the government's answer to the defense's witness request. This is normally set for around a week after the defense's request to give the government time to contact the witnesses and determine if they are going to produce them and at least a week before motions are due since if the government denies any witnesses, the defense will often file a motion requesting that the court order them produced.

The next milestone is the motions due date. A motion is a formal request by one side or the other for the court to rule on a legal issue. Common motions are motions to compel productions of witnesses, motions to suppress, motions to dismiss, and motions for a ruling on an evidentiary issue. Most motions are filed by the defense, but the prosecution sometimes files motions as well. Motions are served on the court and on the opposing counsel.

If the other party opposes any motion, they must do so in writing. A due date for responses to motions is set around a week or two from when the motions were due. Responses to motions are also served on the opposing counsel and the court.

The court will then set a date to hear the motions. The motions hearing is a 39a hearing. A 39a hearing is a hearing on the record that takes place outside the presence of the members. The military courts do not use sidebars, a practice used in some civilian courts where the attorneys come up to the judge's bench and discuss a matter in a low voice so that the jury cannot hear it. Anytime something needs to be discussed that the members should not hear, they are dismissed from the room and a 39a session is held. The 39a sessions are the military equivalent of a sidebar. All that is said is taken down verbatim for the record of trial; however, the members are not present and are not normally told what occurs in the 39a session. Off-the-record sessions with the military judge and the attorneys are called *802 conferences,* from the Rule for Courts-Martial 802 which governs them. What is said in an 802 conference should be summarized by the military judge, with the attorneys having the option to comment on the judge's summary, at the next 39a session.

At the motions hearing, each side will first present their evidence in support of their motions, which may be done through live witness testimony, telephonic testimony, documents, or real evidence such as an alleged murder weapon. The other side will then have the opportunity to present any evidence they have supporting their opposition to the motion via the same formats. Of note, the rules of evidence do not apply at motions hearings, with a few limited exceptions, so things that are inadmissible at trial, such as hearsay, are often considered for purposes of motions. An accused also has the option of testifying for the limited purpose of a particular motion or motions without subjecting himself to any cross-examination on the offenses he is alleged to have committed and without the member's being informed of his testimony. After the presentation of evidence, the party with the burden of proof** will make oral argument followed by the opposing side's argument. Often the judge will give each side the option to respond to specific argument raised by the other side, so the arguments may go back and forth several times much like a debate. The military judge completely controls the format for oral argument and is not required to allow oral argument at all, but it is extremely rare for a judge to deny it when it is requested.

**Generally the moving party, that is, the side filing the motion.

After argument, the military judge makes his ruling. Depending on the complexity of the issue and whether the military judge needs to do additional research, he may make a ruling on the spot orally or he may delay making a ruling and issue a formal, written ruling. Usually, a military judge's ruling cannot be appealed until after the trial; however, either side can request the military judge to reconsider his ruling. Unless additional evidence is discovered, it is unusual for a military judge to reconsider a ruling.

After the motions are heard, the defense will also formally enter pleas and select a forum. However, an accused will almost always select a trial by members even if he intends to be tried by a military judge alone so that he can see what members he would have and which military judge is assigned to the case for the trial. Ideally the same military judge will preside over the trial that presided over the motions hearing but there is no requirement that the same military judge preside over the trial. If the military judge that presided over the motions hearing is unavailable, a second military judge will be detailed for the trial. When an accused in uncertain as to his preferred forum, he should elect members at the motion hearing since a request to change from a members trial to a military-judge-alone trial is usually granted without question up until the time that the trial actually starts; whereas, a request to change to a members trial can delay a trial while members are selected, so a military judge is less likely to allow that change to be made.

After the motions hearing,* unless the military judge dismisses the case or the convening authority withdraws the case, the case will then proceed to trial.

*Sometimes in complicated cases, there are multiple motions hearings.

Sometimes the convening authority will dismiss a case after the motions hearing. This is usually done in one of two situations. The first is if the defense wins key motions that make it unlikely that the government will win at trial. For instance, I had a child molestation case where the military judge ruled that the government would not be able to present expert testimony that amounted to the expert's opinion that the child in question had in fact been molested by my client and that several statements made by the child to other people were hearsay and inadmissible and that I would be able to present evidence that the alleged victim had been molested by another man previously. After the military judge's rulings, the convening authority withdrew the charges since he felt that he was now unlikely to win at trial. Secondly, the convening authority may also dismiss a case if the defense wins motions that will make the case very expensive to try. The convening authority bears the cost of prosecuting the case and sometimes will dismiss a case that he feels he would win on a cost-benefit analysis. This usually happens either when the military judge orders that the government produce a very expensive expert or when he requires the production of a vast number of witnesses. This happened in a couple of cases I had where the military judge required the production of dozens of former recruits from places as far-fetched as Iraq who were present for instances of alleged recruit abuse in drill instructor abuse cases. Rather than pay to fly dozens of witness to San Diego, the convening authority chose to handle the case administratively instead of criminally. Obviously, sometimes the convening authority will take a case to trial despite a very high price associated with the trial, and the more serious the charges, the more likely he is to do so.

The first thing that occurs at the trial is the seating of the members, unless of course the accused has elected to be tried by the military judge alone. Prior to the trial, the government will have sent out a questionnaire to all the members that the convening authority selected for the trial. The questionnaires contain general information such as age, gender, marital status, billet, past duty stations, whether they have been a member before, whether they have ever been the victim of a crime, and so on. Upon reviewing the questionnaires, both trial counsel and defense counsel will submit to the court and each other proposed voir dire, or questions that are asked of members, or juries, to determine whether they should hear a particular case. The military judge will rule on what questions he will allow each side to ask the members en banc, that is, to the entire panel. The en banc questions are yes-or-no questions and the members are instructed to raise their hand if the answer to a question is yes. Since everything that occurs in the court must be recorded as part of the record of trial, the individual asking the question will state what each member's answer is for the record.* Some military judges ask all the en banc questions themselves, but most military judges just ask the standard voir dire questions out of the *Military Judges' Benchbook*** and allow counsel for each side to ask their approved questions.

> *There is a court reporter present who records every word that is spoken on the record.
>
> **Questions such as, "Is there any reason you cannot be an impartial member in this case?" "Will you follow all the military judge's instructions?" "Have you heard anything about this case?" etc.

If any of the en banc responses or the responses on the court-martial questionnaire raises a potential issue about a member, the military judge will then bring that member in for individual voir dire, or questioning. Often the entire panel is brought in one at a time for individual voir dire. Again, the military judge may ask all or the majority of the questions, or he may allow counsel to ask the questions; the military judge has very broad discretion in how voir dire is conducted and in what questions are asked. In individual voir dire, the members are asked regular questions and then respond verbally.

At the completion of the voir dire, the military judge will then allow each side to make any challenges for cause that they have against a member. Challenges for cause are granted when a member has some bias or appears to have some bias that will affect his ability to sit as a fair and impartial member in that court-martial. The military judge may also *sua sponte*, or on his own without being asked, dismiss a member if in his opinion the member should be dismissed, even if neither side challenged the member. This is usually only done when an attorney misses challenging someone that the military judge believes clearly should have been challenged, and that if the military judge leaves the member on the panel, the impartiality of the members panel would be seriously compromised.

After the military judge rules on the challenges for cause, he will then hear any peremptory challenge. Each side has one peremptory challenge that he may use to remove any member for no stated reason, except that the reason for removing the member may not be because of his race or gender. If the other party feels that a member is having a peremptory challenge exercised against him based on race or gender, the party may request that the military judge require the side exercising the challenge to state a race- and gender-neutral reason for exercising the challenge, and the military judge will usually grant that request. If the attorney cannot state a reasonable race- and gender-neutral reason for the challenge, the military judge will not allow the attorney to exercise the peremptory challenge.

Sometimes after the military judge grants the challenges, there are not enough members, called a *quorum*, left to proceed. This is called *busting* or *breaking quorum*. When this happens, the military judge will dismiss all the members and continue the case long enough to allow the convening authority to appoint a new members panel and the court will proceed with voir dire on the new panel.

If a quorum of members remains, the military judge will call in the members, dismiss the ones that he granted challenges on, and the case will precede.

The military judge will then give the members their preliminary instructions. These include how to properly conduct themselves as members, that the burden of proof is on the government, and so on. These are standard instructions out of the *Military Judges' Benchbook*, and the military judge rarely deviates from them, although either party may ask the military judge to modify them for a particular case.

Next, the trial counsel will give his opening statement. Opening statements are supposed to be a summary of the evidence that the members will hear and see. However, if the other party does not object, many military judges will allow a fair amount of argument in the opening as well.

The defense counsel usually gives his opening statement immediately after the trial counsel gives his; however, the rules do allow the defense to reserve their opening statement until after the government rests, that is, finishes its case.

Next, the government is given the opportunity to present its case. The initial presentation of a case is called the *case in chief*. The government can present its case through witness testimony, physical evidence, stipulation of fact, and judicial notice. A stipulation of fact is an agreement between counsel for both sides and the accused that a certain fact or facts is true and cannot be contradicted. Most trials do not contain stipulations of fact, but most guilty pleas do. A stipulation of fact is a tool that speeds up a trial and makes it unnecessary to call the witness that would testify about the fact. Sometimes the convening authority will allow an accused to enter into a pretrial agreement where pleas of not guilty are entered and the case goes to trial, but in exchange for the stipulation of fact, the confinement will be capped at a certain amount if the accused is found guilty. This is usually done with lengthy scientific evidence that would require a very expensive expert to present. Judicial notice is when the court recognizes a fact as true. Judicial notice is only taken when a fact is not subject to reasonable dispute and can be readily proved a source whose accuracy cannot reasonably be questioned. Common examples of judicial notice include what day of the week a specific day was on, what time sunrise was on a specific day, and so on. Members are not required to accept a judicially noticed fact as true.

After the government finishes presenting its case, it rests. When the government rests, the defense is given the opportunity to request a finding of not guilty on any specific charge. This is called a *917 motion* because Rule for Courts-Martial (RCM) 917 contains the procedure for this request. A finding of not guilty is only entered if the government fails to present any evidence on an element of a charge. Ideally, the government should never refer a charge if it cannot present evidence in support of all of the charge's elements; however, it is not unusual for the defense to win a 917 motion. This is because sometimes witnesses change their testimony, most military attorneys are inexperienced and make mistakes at trial, and because the convening authority chooses what charges go to trial and the convening authority does not always listen to his attorneys and may refer charges that there is no evidence to support.

After the military judge rules on any 917 motions, unless he dismisses all charges, the defense has the opportunity to present a case. The defense can present evidence using the same methods that the government is allowed to use. The defense is not required to present a case, but it is somewhat unusual for the defense not to present anything. I have personally only done this one time, and it was because I was as certain as is possible to be in a trial that the members were ready to acquit my client, and I did not want to present any evidence, because it could have made them change their minds. I was correct, and the accused was acquitted. But I can assure you that I was second guessing myself during the entire deliberations!

If the defense chooses to present a case, upon the conclusion of their case, the government will be given the opportunity to present a case in rebuttal. The government is only allowed to present evidence that rebuts evidence that the defense presented in its case in chief. The defense is then given the opportunity to present a case in surrebuttal to rebut anything from the government's case in rebuttal. It is pretty rare to see a case in surrebuttal.

After the both sides have concluded their presentation of evidence, closing arguments are generally given. Some military judges give the members their instructions on reaching a finding (rendering a verdict) before closing arguments to allow counsel the opportunity to work the instructions into their arguments; however, most military judges generally have closing arguments and then give the instructions. The government gives their closing argument first, and then the defense gives theirs. After the defense gives their closing argument, the government is permitted a final rebuttal argument.

After the closing arguments, the members are given their instructions, if they have not received them yet. The instructions are the military judge's guidance to the members on how to reach their verdict. They include general rules on how deliberations are carried out; what elements, or facts, the members must find beyond a reasonable doubt to convict the accused on any charge; what defenses may apply and what facts the members would have to find for the defense to apply; and how to interpret the evidence. The instructions can be a very important part of the case, especially if the defense has raised an affirmative defense, such as mistake of fact, entrapment, or insanity. The *Military Judges' Benchbook* is a guide used by the military judge in overseeing the trial. It also contains a long list of members' instructions and indicates in which situation they may be appropriate. Both sides pick which instructions that they feel apply to the case and request the military judge to give them. Each side also has the opportunity to draft their own instructions if they can find a law or case that supports their requested instruction, but that is rarely done as the benchbook is quite exhaustive and military judges are generally loath to give novel instructions for fear of creating unnecessary appellate issues.

The court is then closed for the members' deliberation. Deliberations often only last a few hours in the military but can take many days in certain complicated cases. Deliberations are much shorter than in the civilian justice system because a unanimous verdict is not required* and there is no such thing as a hung members' panel on the merits. Most civilian court systems require a unanimous verdict, thus the civilian jury continues to vote and deliberate until they all vote guilty or they all vote not guilty. If they are unable to reach a unanimous verdict, the judge will declare a mistrial, which is called a *hung jury*. The prosecutor then has to decide if he is going to retry the case. In the military system, the members deliberate until they are ready to vote. They vote one time. If two-thirds or more vote guilty, then the verdict is guilty. If less than two-thirds vote guilty, then the verdict is not guilty. Members do not redeliberate and revote until a unanimous verdict is reached. There is a procedure where after the vote has been taken but before it is announced in court that the members may request permission of the military judge to revote; this is called *reconsidering the verdict*. This, however, is extremely rare, and in cases of a revote, the same rules apply for whether the verdict is guilty or not guilty. There is no continued revoting until a unanimous verdict is reached.

*Only a two-thirds vote is required for a guilty verdict.

If a verdict of not guilty is given on all charges, then the case is over. If the accused is found guilty on any charge, then there is a sentencing hearing.

The government is given the opportunity to present any evidence in aggravation, such as the effect the crime had on the victim or the service member's unit.

The defense is then given the opportunity to present any matters in extenuation or mitigation, that is, things that explain why an accused committed a crime or why he should not be punished as harshly for the crime he committed. Usually, the defense is given pretty great latitude to present pretty much any evidence that they want to. The defense may also relax the rules of evidence so that they may present things such as letters or take testimony telephonically. If the defense relaxes the rules of evidence, then the rules are relaxed for the government as well and the government may present evidence using the same relaxed format during their case in rebuttal. Just as in the merits phase of the trial, the accused has the option to make a statement or to remain silent. However, unlike during the merits, if the accused elects to make a statement, he may make either a sworn or an unsworn statement. If he makes a sworn statement he may be cross-examined. If the accused makes as unsworn statement, then he cannot be cross-examined. An unsworn statement may be made verbally, in writing, or through counsel. Usually an accused will make an unsworn statement.

Just as during the case on the merits, during the sentencing case, after the defense is finished presenting its sentencing evidence, the government has the opportunity to present a case in rebuttal and the defense may then present a case in surrebuttal.

After all the evidence is presented, the government argues for what it believes is an appropriate sentence and then the defense is given an opportunity to make a sentencing argument. The government does not get to make a second argument at sentencing.

After argument, the members are instructed on sentencing procedures. Just as with the findings instructions, the counsel are given the opportunity to request specific sentencing instructions. However, sentencing instructions are usually very standard and differ little from case to case except that the maximum sentence is different from case to case.

The members will then close to deliberate on the sentence. To adjudge a sentence of ten years or less, two-thirds of the members must agree. To adjudge a sentence of more than ten years, three-fourths of the members must agree, unless the sentence is death in which case all the members must agree. The members deliberate, and after they have finished deliberating, each member may propose a sentence. All the proposed sentences are written down and given to the president of the panel, who is the senior member. He is the military equivalent of the foreperson of a jury. He will then arrange the sentences from least to most severe. The panel will vote on each sentence starting with the least severe until the required majority is reached for a particular sentence. If no proposed sentence is accepted by the required majority, the panel deliberates again and then revotes. This process continues until a sentence is reached.

If the sentence includes any confinement the accused is immediately taken to the brig. Reductions in rank and forfeitures of pay ordinarily take place fourteen days later. Any punitive discharge must be reviewed and approved by the appellate courts before it can be enacted. There are three types of punitive discharges: a bad-conduct discharge (BCD), a dishonorable discharge (DD), and a dismissal. A dishonorable discharge can only be awarded by a general court-martial. Only officers can be awarded a dismissal,* and a dismissal can only be awarded by a general court-martial.

*An officer cannot be given a dishonorable discharge or a bad-conduct discharge.

During the court-martial, the court reporter records every word that is spoken on the record. If the accused is acquitted, he is provided a summarized record of trial (ROT). The testimony of each witness is summarized and the arguments are left out. If the accused is convicted but not sentenced to a punitive discharge or a year or more of confinement, he is also given a summarized record of trial. If he is sentenced to a punitive discharge or over a year of confinement, then a verbatim record of trial is prepared. It includes every word that is spoken on the record during the court-martial.

After the record of trial is prepared, it is served on the defense and it has the opportunity to bring up any mistakes in the transcription. The record of trial is also sent to the staff judge advocate who drafts up his recommendations to the convening authority on what to do with the case post-trial. This is called the *staff judge advocate's recommendation* (SJAR). The staff judge advocate's recommendation contains the staff judge advocate's comments on any allegation of errors made at trial raised by the defense and what punishment the staff judge advocate recommends that the convening authority approve. Generally the staff judge advocate recommends that the convening authority approve the maximum possible sentence, that is, the sentence given at the court-martial.

Any time after the conclusion of the court-martial until ten days after the staff judge advocate's recommendation is served on the defense, the defense can submit a clemency request to the convening authority. In a clemency request, the defense can request that the convening authority give a lesser sentence than the court-martial adjudged. The convening authority is the one that actually approves the conviction and the sentence. He can always disapprove any conviction or sentence. The convening authority can never increase the punishment from the court-martial but he can always lessen it. Likewise, he can change a finding of guilty to not guilty but not vice versa.

After the convening authority receives the staff judge advocate's recommendation, the record of trial, and the clemency request, if one is submitted, he acts on the case; that is, he approves or disapproves the conviction and sentence. Once the convening authority acts, the detailed defense counsel is relieved from the case.

If the sentence as approved includes either a punitive discharge or a year or more of confinement, the case is automatically appealed to the service's court of criminal appeals. The accused is assigned as appellate defense counsel. Appellate defense counsel are judge advocates, and they are not the same judge advocate who served as the trial defense counsel. The accused also has the right to hire a civilian attorney to represent him on appeal. The appellate court can affirm the lower court, dismiss the case, order it to be retried, or reduce the sentence. Punitive discharges must be approved by the first-level appellate court* and cannot be given until the appellate court reviews the case. If the defendant is released from the brig before his case is reviewed, he will most likely be placed on appellate leave. Appellate leave is a status that service members can be placed on while pending a punitive discharge. While on appellate leave a service member is still technically in the military but he does not work for the military and he is not paid. However, the service member still gets medical coverage and has access to commissaries, exchanges, base gyms, and so on.

> *The court of criminal appeals for the particular branch, i.e., the Navy-Marine Corps Court of Criminal Appeals, the Army Court of Criminal Appeals, etc.

If the sentence as approved by the convening authority does not include a punitive discharge or confinement for over a year, the accused can still file a request that an appeal be heard on his case through the judge advocate general.

The appropriate court of criminal appeals has several options when it hears a case. It can find the trial court acted correctly and affirm the convening authority's action, it can find the trial court made an error but that the error was harmless and thus still affirm the convening authority's action, it can send the case back to the trial court to consider a specific matter, it can reverse the case and send it back to the convening authority, it can lessen the punishment approved by the convening authority, or it can dismiss the case and not allow the convening authority to refer it again.*

*Called *dismissing a case with prejudice.*

If the accused wishes, he may appeal the decision of the court of criminal appeals to the Court of Appeals for the Armed Forces (CAAF). The Court of Appeals for the Armed Forces hears appeals from each of the armed services' courts of criminal appeals. The military may or may not help with an appeal to the Court of Appeals for the Armed Forces. If the appellate defense counsel believes that there is a good issue to appeal to the Court of Appeals for the Armed Forces, he will assist the accused in such an appeal. Otherwise, the accused will have to proceed on his own. He can hire a civilian counsel to make the appeal or he can represent himself.

The Court of Appeals for the Armed Forces can do anything that the courts of criminal appeals can do. The Court of Appeals for the Armed Forces may also send the case back to the court of criminal appeals to consider a certain issue.

A ruling from the Court of Appeals for the Armed Forces can be appealed to the United States Supreme Court. The military does not assist in appeals to the Supreme Court, and it is rare that the Supreme Court grants certiorari (agrees to hear) to a military appeal.

In certain instances, an accused can also file a writ of habeas corpus in federal district court. This is extremely rare. The request must allege that the accused is being confined in violation of his constitutional rights and that the issue cannot or was not resolved by the normal appellate process. Military attorneys do not assist in filing such writs. The denial of a writ of habeas corpus may be appealed to the federal circuit court the district court falls under and from there to the United States Supreme Court.

I have never personally seen a writ of habeas corpus filed in a military case. There was one case where I was considering filing a writ of habeas corpus. When I was on active duty, I represented a service member in a war crimes case. He, along with other service members, was alleged to have kidnapped an Iraqi, planted evidence to make it look like he was planting an improvised explosive device (IED), a common booby trap used by insurgents in Iraq, and then to have shot and killed him. These allegations came at almost the same time as allegations that Marines had killed twenty-four civilians at Haditha after the Marines were hit by an IED. My client and the other service members that were charged with him were all immediately placed in pretrial confinement, while the Haditha Marines were not. The military does not have bail, so the service members faced the prospect of very lengthy periods of pretrial confinement while their defense teams prepared to take these difficult cases to trial. My client filed a request with the military judge to release him from pretrial confinement. The military judge denied the request. I considered enlisting the aid of my wife, Kristy Callahan, an attorney who was in private practice at the time and who was admitted before the federal district court that has jurisdiction over the Pendleton brig where my client was held, to file the writ of habeas corpus on my client's behalf since I could not file the request. None of the military prosecutors handling the case were admitted before that federal court, so I do not know how the Marine Corps would have handled the issue since they are so rare. I got the idea because Lt. Calley, who was charged with war crimes from Vietnam that occurred at My Lai, had filed a similar habeas corpus appeal. However the request for a writ of habeas corpus was never filed because a pretrial agreement (PTA) was reached in the case. My client agreed to plead guilty in exchange for the government dropping the more serious charges and limiting the amount of confinement that he would serve.

In addition to the appeals process, the military also has a parole process, as do civilian justice systems. The Navy Clemency and Parole Board (NC&PB) handles Marine Corps and Navy cases. The Navy Clemency and Parole Board is comprised of five officers, and they are not required to be judge advocates. The Navy Clemency and Parole Board reviews cases for the first time after the accused has been in confinement for a year and reviews them every year. In many cases, the Navy Clemency and Parole Board only makes recommendation to the secretary of the Navy, and he makes the final decision. As in civilian justice systems, a significant number of service members are given parole. The Navy Clemency and Parole Board also has limited authority to grant clemency and can also recommend the secretary of the Navy grant clemency. However, unlike parole, clemency is very rarely granted.

ADVERSE ADMINISTRATIVE ACTIONS

In addition to criminal proceedings, there are a variety of adverse administrative actions that the military can initiate against service members. Some of these administrative actions are uniquely military, and some of them are similar to ones that exist in civilian employment. Service members are entitled to be represented by counsel for some of these proceedings and are always entitled to speak with military counsel about them.

Because of various levels of defense counsel involvement with these issues, they are often mistaken for criminal matters. However, since they are administrative, and not criminal, in nature, many of the protections that apply in criminal proceeding do not apply. The biggest differences between administrative matters and criminal matters are that in administrative matters, the rules of evidence do not apply, the exclusionary rule does not apply, and the standard of proof is a preponderance of the evidence instead of proof beyond a reasonable doubt.* Therefore, things such as hearsay that are inadmissible in a court-martial can be used for these proceedings. Likewise, evidence that was obtained in violation of the service member's constitutional rights may still be used against him. Sometimes serious criminal charges that could not be proved at court beyond a reasonable doubt or where the evidence has been suppressed under the exclusionary rule are sent to administrative forums because it is easier for the military to win at an administrative hearing.

> *The exclusionary rule requires that certain evidence be kept out, or excluded, from criminal proceedings. It is a rule created by the Supreme Court to remedy certain constitutional violations of a defendant's rights by the government. The most common violations that trigger the exclusionary rule are questioning an individual without informing them of their rights and seizing evidence without a search warrant in a situation that would legally require a search warrant.

The various administrative actions that can be taken are best broken into two categories: those that are purely a negative personnel record type action and those that are administrative forms of punishment that can result in loss of pay, rank, or liberty. Each branch of the military has its own names for its various adverse administrative actions; however, despite the differences in name, they function pretty much the same.

Administrative actions that only form the basis of evaluations, or that are solely negative marks on a service member's file, include the following: informal counseling, a nonpunitive letter of caution, extra military instruction, formal counseling, an adverse fitness report, and relief for cause. These actions are done by a supervisor in the chain of command of the service member. They are done simply if the supervisor feels that they are appropriate, and generally a service member cannot appeal them except to another person higher up the chain of command than the supervisor taking the action. These types of administrative action do not require judge advocate involvement and normally they do not have judge advocate involvement, but it is not unusual for a service member to get counsel from a judge advocate about these issues. Depending on how busy the judge advocate is (criminal matters and more serious administrative matters always take priority) and on how unjust the judge advocate believes the situation to be, he may provide minor assistance. However, that usually consists just of making recommendations to the service member on how to approach the issue with the chain of command or at most the judge advocate calling the supervisor and arguing that the action being taken is unjust.

The least severe administrative action is an informal counseling. The service member is corrected verbally or in writing by any superior for a perceived deficiency. This is no different than at a civilian place of employment; however, there are always service members that will come and talk to judge advocate about the counseling because the advice of a judge advocate is always free.

A service member can also be given a nonpunitive letter of caution, often referred to as a *niplock*. A nonpunitive letter of caution is more formal and is considered more serious than informal counseling. A nonpunitive letter of caution is not placed in a service member's service record book (SRB) or officer qualification record (OCR). An enlisted member will have a service record book; an officer will have an officer qualification record. Service record books and officer qualification records are the Marine Corps equivalent of a civilian personnel file kept by many employers to record things, both good and bad, about their employees.

A minor administrative tool that is often used is extra military instruction (EMI). Extra military instruction is a specific task typically done before or after working hours. Extra military instruction is not supposed to punish but rather to be used to correct a specific deficiency. For example, if a service member runs slowly, he may be given more running. If he is not performing the technical aspects of his job correctly, he may be required to read manuals or spend extra time practicing a particular skill set. The task given is required by regulations to directly relate to the deficiency and help correct it; however, it is not unusual to see extra military instruction that does not fit this requirement. For instance, although incorrect, a service member may be assigned extra policing (cleaning) duties over the weekend for being disrespectful.

A service member can also be given a formal counseling that will be placed in the service record book or officer qualification record. This is called a *page 11 entry* in the Marine Corps. The formal counseling will be a permanent part of the service member's record and will be reviewed when he is considered for things such as promotion. If the service member receives two or more formal counseling, they may also form the basis for administratively separating the service member. In essence, a formal counseling in the military is not much different than a written complaint placed in a civilian employee's personnel file.

Service members are also given proficiency and conduct markings (pros and cons) or fitness reports, depending on their seniority. In the Marine Corps, E-5s (sergeants) and above are given fitness reports. These are the military equivalent of performance evaluations. There are certain rules that govern when adverse pros and cons or fitness reports may be given, but in practice, pros and cons and fitness reports function very similarly to employee evaluations in the civilian sector. If your supervisor feels that you are doing a bad job, he will give you an adverse performance report.

Lastly, a service member can also be relieved for cause. A relief for cause will be accompanied by an adverse fitness report or pros and cons. A service member is relieved for cause if he is not properly performing the duties of his billet. After he is relieved for cause, he will be assigned another billet. Often if a service member is relieved for cause, it will end his career. He will either not be allowed to reenlist or he will not be promoted.

> *In the military, if service members are not promoted within certain time frames, they are not allowed to continue to serve.

The more serious administrative measures that can result in the loss of pay, rank, or even result in a discharge, are competency review board (CRB), nonjudicial punishment (NJP),* summary court-martial (SCM)* and administrative separation proceedings.

> *Also referred to as *captain's* or *admiral's mast* or *article 15* because it comes from article 15 of the UCMJ.

> **Not to be confused with a special court martial (SPCM), which is an actual criminal court.

A competency review board is an administrative board that has the ability to reduce an enlisted service member one rank. The commanding officer has the authority to send the service member before such a board, which is generally composed of three service members. A service member is not entitled to be represented by counsel at a competency review board. A competency review board is not supposed to be used as a punitive tool, but rather to return a service member to his former rank after he has demonstrated that he is not ready for his current rank. A competency review board is generally convened over maturity or leadership deficiencies.

Nonjudicial punishment is a punitive measure that allows a commanding officer to punish service members for minor criminal infractions. Orders violations, periods of unauthorized absences, adultery, DUIs, and minor assaults are commonly handled at this forum.

Nonjudicial punishment is generally held by the commanding officer, but it may be held by an officer in charge as well. The commanding officer listens to the evidence against the service member as well as any evidence that the service member wishes to present. The commanding officer then decides whether the service member is guilty, using a preponderance of the evidence standard, meaning he does believe that it is more likely than not that the service member committed the offense. There also are no rules of evidence at nonjudicial punishment. The service member is not represented by counsel at the nonjudicial punishment. The service member has the right to refuse nonjudicial punishment, in which case the commanding officer must decide whether to take administrative proceedings that do not require the consent of the service member, to drop the issue, or to send it to a court-martial. A nonjudicial punishment "conviction" is not a criminal conviction.

The maximum punishment that can be given at nonjudicial punishment is relatively minor, and it depends on who is giving the nonjudicial punishment and the rank of the service member that it is imposed on. The most serious punishments that can be given are forfeiture of one-half pay for two months, CCU (correctional custody unit) for thirty days or restriction for sixty days, and reduction of one rank. CCU is similar to being sent back to boot camp. It is not used very often and can only be imposed on junior service members. Usually, a Marine is sent to CCU if the commanding officer believes that the Marine has the potential to be a good Marine but just needs to have a little more discipline instilled in him.

The commanding officer may also send the matter to a summary court-martial (SCM). A summary court-martial is still an administrative proceeding and should not be confused with a special or general court-martial, which are both criminal proceedings. A service member also has the right to refuse a summary court-martial. A summary court-martial is convened by the commanding officer. He determines the charges, and he appoints an officer in his command to serve as the summary court-martial officer. The summary court-martial officer serves as judge, prosecuting attorney, and defense attorney. He is supposed to examine and develop the evidence for both sides. The punishment that he can give is significantly higher than the punishment that may be given at nonjudicial punishment. Unlike at nonjudicial punishment, the rules of evidence do apply; however, since the summary court-martial officer is rarely an attorney, they are not usually strictly followed. The standard of proof is beyond a reasonable doubt. However, this is still not a criminal proceeding, and conviction does not result in a criminal conviction since the service member is not represented by counsel. An important item to note is that although an individual is not represented by military counsel at a summary court-martial, and judge advocates will merely give advice on how to proceed, the service member may obtain a civilian counsel, which the summary court-martial officer will sometimes allow to represent the accused at the hearing. Generally speaking this is a bad idea as some states may consider a summary court-martial conviction a criminal conviction if the accused is represented by counsel at the proceeding. Before a service member has an attorney represent him at a summary court-martial, he should carefully discuss the matter with both the civilian attorney and a judge advocate. As is the case with non-judicial punishment, if the service member refuses the summary court-martial, the commanding officer must decide whether to take administrative proceedings that do not require the consent of the service member, or to drop the issue, or to send it to a court-martial (special or general).

The punishment that can be given at a summary court-martial is also minor and depends on the rank of the service member receiving the summary court-martial. The maximum possible punishment that can be given at a summary court-martial is confinement for thirty days, forfeiture of two-thirds pay for a month and reduction in rank.

Lastly, there is the process of administrative separation (commonly referred to as an *adsep*). Administrative separation proceedings are a method for discharging a service member before his contract is over. Administrative separation proceedings do not require the consent of the service member and can be initiated over his objection. There are three different characterizations of service that can result from administrative separation proceedings; from most favorable to least favorable, they are an honorable discharge, a general discharge,* and an other-than-honorable discharge (OTH). A bad-conduct discharge or a dishonorable discharge may not be given as they are punitive discharges and can only be awarded by a court-martial.

> *Also called a *general discharge under honorable conditions.*

Administrative separation proceedings fall into two categories: those that require an administrative separation board (commonly referred to as a board) and those that do not. Generally, if the government is seeking to separate someone with an other-than-honorable discharge or someone that has over six years of service, then a board will be required.

There are many different reasons that a service member may be separated; however, the most common reasons are for the commission of a serious offense or for a pattern of misconduct.

Administrative separation proceedings are generally initiated by a commanding officer.* If a board is required, the commanding officer will appoint the board which consists of three members: generally, one field-grade officer to serve as the president of the board, a company-grade officer, and a senior enlisted member.

> *In some instances, the proceedings may be initiated by a higher command.

Service members have the right to be represented by counsel at the board, and judge advocates are appointed to serve as defense counsel for administrative-separation cases that require a board. The government is represented by a recorder. The recorder is not required to be an attorney, and generally he is not. Most bases have a chief warrant officer that serves as the officer in charge of the administrative (admin) law section,* and he serves as the recorder for all boards.

> *The section responsible for processing administrative separations.

A legal advisor is also appointed to the board, but he has no actual authority. He is generally the deputy staff judge advocate. It always frustrated me that a judge advocate working for the commanding officer trying to separate the service member serves as the legal advisor to the board.

The service member that the government is attempting to separate is called the *respondent*. The respondent has rights at the board that are similar to the rights afforded at criminal proceedings; the most significant of which are the rights to see all the evidence against him, to know who the government witnesses are going to be, to cross-examine all witnesses called, and to present evidence on his own behalf. The respondent may remain silent, or he may make either a sworn or an unsworn statement. If he makes a sworn statement, he can be cross-examined by the recorder, and the board may ask him questions as well. If he chooses to make an unsworn statement, then he cannot be questioned by either.

Boards are conducted much like trials, except that there are no rules of evidence and the government can present evidence that would be excluded from a criminal trial under the exclusionary rule. The board opens with the president of the board formally informing the respondent of his rights before the board. Both sides are then given the opportunity to voir dire (question) the members of the board and to make any challenges for cause that either side believes are appropriate. The government will then be allowed to make an opening statement, followed by the defense. The government will then be permitted to put on their case, followed by the defense. The respondent has the right to make a sworn statement (in which case he can be cross-examined by the recorder and the members may question his as well) and an unsworn statement (in which case he is not subject to being cross-examined), and he also has the right to remain silent. After the defense rests, the government may put on a case in rebuttal, and if they do, the defense may then present a case in surrebuttal. Both sides will then make closing arguments. The government argues first and is allowed to make a rebuttal argument after the defense makes their closing argument.

The board will then deliberate. The burden of proof is on the government by a preponderance of the evidence. A majority vote, or two members, is required for any finding. First, the board must determine whether the alleged conduct occurred. If the board finds that it did, they must next determine whether or not it warrants separating the service member. If the board finds that separation is warranted, they will recommend the character of service.

While the board is in session, there is a recording device in place. A summary of the testimony at the board along with any physical or documentary evidence will be sent to the separation authority.

The results of the board are then sent to the separation authority, who is generally the first general or admiral up the chain of command and who is also the general court-martial convening authority. The separation authority has the authority to approve any lesser discharge than the one recommended by the board. He also has the authority to not separate or suspend any recommended separation. In certain circumstances, the separation authority can separate when no separation was recommended, but such requests must be sent to the office of the Secretary of the Navy for approval. It is rare that the separation authority will seek to separate a service member when the board recommends that the service member be retained.

Administrative separation proceedings for an officer are slightly different. The board is called a *board of inquiry* (BOI) and is sometimes referred to as a show-cause hearing because the paperwork notifying the officer of the board of inquiry states that he is to appear and show cause why he should be retained in the armed services. However, despite that language, the burden of proof is still on the government by a preponderance of the evidence. The authority to separate an officer is also significantly further up the chain of command.

INJUSTICES

In this section, specific problems of the military justice system are discussed in detail. Also included is a recommended way to correct each injustice.

CONVENING AUTHORITY INJUSTICES

The next several chapters deal with problems with the convening authority. For years, the power of the convening authority has been frequently cited as fraught with peril due to the potential for abuse. Unfortunately, the congress, the president, and the armed forces have done very little to correct the situation. The obvious solution to this problem is to replace the convening authority with a district attorney–type figure. This practical and effective solution is explored in detail in the chapter "The Solution to the Convening Authority Injustices" after the individual problems with the convening authority are addressed.

The Convening Authority Refers Cases to Trial

The first problem with the convening authority is that he alone has the authority to refer a case to a court-martial, that is to press charges. The convening authority is a commanding officer and is usually at least a lieutenant colonel (O-5). The convening authority can be of any military occupational specialty (MOS) and is only very rarely an attorney.

There are two types of convening authorities: those with special court-martial convening authority, and those with general court-martial convening authority. Generally, a battalion commander (most commonly a lieutenant colonel), or equivalent-sized unit commander, is the special court-martial convening authority. The division commanding general, or equivalent-sized unit commander, is the general court-martial convening authority. A special court-martial is the military equivalent of a misdemeanor court. The maximum punishment is confinement for one year, forfeiture of two-thirds pay due per month for a period of twelve months, reduction to the lowest enlisted pay grade, and discharge with a bad-conduct discharge. A general court-martial is the military equivalent of a felony court. It can award any punishment authorized for an offense up to and including death. Total forfeitures and a dishonorable discharge may also be awarded. Officers cannot be given a bad-conduct discharge or a dishonorable discharge; they can only be dismissed.

A general court-martial convening authority normally has served at least twenty years in the military, and a special court-martial convening authority normally has served at least fifteen years. Most general court-martial convening authorities will have several special court-martial convening authorities under their command.

Allowing the convening authority to decide whether to charge a service member—and if so, what charges to bring—creates problems on both ends of the justice spectrum. On one hand, there are convening authorities who bring charges that lack merit, and on the other hand, there are convening authorities who do not refer charges that justice demands an individual be held accountable for. It is more common to see a convening authority bringing charges that lack merit than it is to see a convening authority not bring charges that he should, but both extremes are wrong, and a justice system should be designed to prevent both.

There are three primary reasons that convening authorities tend to commit injustices when referring cases to trial. First and foremost, they are not attorneys. Nowhere else in America do we allow nonattorneys to send charges to court. The convening authority can be anything from an infantry officer to a supply officer. Most of them do not have an education above a master's degree, and the master's degree is often from a military school such as the Army War College or the Naval Postgraduate School and is in a military subject. Convening authorities frequently have little or no training in the law. Until they become a convening authority, they usually have little to no interaction with the law. We then allow these individuals who often have no formal legal training and very little legal experience to make very important and sometimes literally life-or-death legal decisions. Most military leaders would never dream of letting a judge advocate command an infantry division in combat, and rightfully so, because the judge advocate lacks the training and twenty-plus years of infantry experience that a division commanding general has. So why do the same military leaders believe that it is a good idea to allow the infantry general to make legal decisions that permanently alter the lives of both those accused and of those who are victims without the education, training, and years of experience that a judge advocate has? Allowing the convening authority to make the decision to refer a case to trial is a fundamental flaw in the military justice system and one that will cause injustice upon injustice as long as it is allowed to continue.

Secondly, the convening authority often knows the accused. The accused is a service member that works for him. A special court-martial convening authority is much more likely to know the accused because he will have a much smaller command, but even the general court-martial convening authority sometimes knows the accused. The more senior the accused is, the more likely it is that the convening authority will know him.

Allowing the convening authority to refer charges against individuals he knows has problems at both extremes. If the convening authority likes the individual, he may refer lesser charges that than justice would require, or he may not refer any charges at all. On the other hand, if he dislikes the service member, he may refer charges when he should not or he may refer more serious charges than justice warrants. The power to refer charges is an incredible power. It is one that has the potential to forever change many lives, either for the better or for the worse. It should never be exercised in a situation where personal feelings can influence its use. I personally represented dozens of clients that the convening authority knew well. On the civilian side, most people would never feel comfortable allowing a boss in their company to decide whether to send them to trial. It has always left me feeling uneasy knowing that I could be sent to a court-martial by my convening authority since I usually had rocky relations with most of the commanding officers that I had. These poor relations were caused by my zealous representation of other Marines within the same command as mine, but that is another injustice for another chapter and is discussed in the chapter "Government Control of Defense Counsel."

A third reason that allowing the convening authority to refer charges frequently results in injustices is because the convening authority can often have a nonofficial interest in the outcome of the case. This nonofficial interest usually arises in one of three different situations. First, in the military, the commanding officer is often viewed as responsible, to varying degrees, for all that occurs or fails to occur in his unit. Sometimes this results in a convening authority referring charges to cover up poor leadership or dereliction on his own part. As an example of poor leadership and dereliction, I represented a Marine at a general court-martial on charges that included manslaughter. He was a drill instructor. This Marine was responsible for teaching other drill instructors how to train recruits in the pool. This Marine's job was quite important since the drill instructors that he trained would then train the recruits to swim and even how to swim with combat gear. These are obviously essential skills for Marines, and many recruits come to boot camp either not knowing how to swim at all or swimming very poorly. The task is compounded because these recruits must be taught to swim while wearing a substantial amount of heavy gear. Some recruits when placed in the water, especially with gear, lose control and, out of fear of drowning, trash about wildly and grab on to anything or anyone near them. These recruits can drown themselves or grab and drown other recruits as well. The Marine Corps had a rigorous program to train the drill instructors that work at the pool to deal with such situations and to ensure that recruits do not harm themselves or other recruits while in the pool.

My client was one of multiple drill instructors who were training a particular trainee drill instructor when the student died in the water. My client had tried to get the other drill instructor dropped from the course because he was not a good enough swimmer for the course, but the command did not allow him to be dropped from the course. My client was ordered to complete the other drill instructors' training. My client carried out the order and followed through with the rigorous training. He used the same methods and techniques that the command had taught him to use. Unfortunately, while the trainee Drill Instructor was treading the water after a rigorous workout, he passed out. My client immediately retrieved him from the pool (he was in the water next to the trainee drill instructor) and attempted to revive him. The trainee drill instructor briefly seemed to regain consciousness, but then died. There was some dispute as to what caused the drill instructor to die. However, most of the expert testimony at trial pointed to shallow-water blackout as the cause of death. Shallow-water blackout occurs when someone's head is not underwater, but enough water has accumulated in their lungs that the individual is not able to get enough oxygen to the brain during periods of exertion and passes out and then dies. This is also called *dry-land drowning*. The trainee drill instructor's head was not underwater when he passed out, but he had spent a lot of time in the pool that day and a lot of time under the water. He was also being placed under extreme physical exertion, as was required by the program. The drill instructor's death was tragic, but my client was only training him as he was ordered to and in the way that he had been taught to.

Charges were referred against multiple instructors to include my client, and he was sent to an article 32 hearing. At the conclusion of the hearing, the investigating officer recommended that all charges be dismissed, citing that my client was only doing what he had been ordered to do in the way he had been taught to do it and that my client had no idea that the training could be lethal. The investigating officer further blamed the command for establishing a faulty and dangerous program.

The convening authority, the commanding general of the command that the investigating officer found to be at fault, referred the case to a trial on charges that included manslaughter despite the recommendations of the investigating officer. Personally, I have always suspected that the decision to refer that case to trial was motivated, at least in part, by a desire to cover up errors in the program and to protect senior members of the command and the Marine Corps from facing criticism for their leadership failure and dereliction for failing to properly create a safe training program. It was much easier to lay the blame for the death at the feet of my client than to admit that the command, the convening authority, and even the institution of the Marine Corps, had failed the deceased drill instructor.

My client was in fact tried and was acquitted of all charges. After his trial, I had the privilege of conducting his promotion ceremony. He was and is an outstanding Marine. I firmly believe that the Corps let him down by making him and his family endure the agony of a trial in which he faced many years of confinement.

Anytime a situation such as that one arises, there will always be the temptation for a convening authority to take the easy way out and refer charges against a Marine to protect his command image and the institution of the Marine Corps. It is much easier to say a rouge Marine committed a crime and that is the reason for whatever tragic incident occurred than it is for the convening authority to admit that as the commanding officer he failed to properly lead and supervise his unit. This temptation to deflect blame must be removed.

A second situation that arises in which the convening authority has a nonofficial interest in the outcome of the case arises when he is attempting to cover up criminal conduct of his own. This does not happen as often as attempting to cover up poor leadership or dereliction, which can also be a criminal charge in the military. I had a case where I was representing a senior enlisted Marine for adultery charges. What generally happens with such cases, at least in the Marine Corps, is that the Marine is given nonjudicial punishment and forced to retire. The convening authority in this case (it was a special court-martial) refused to give the Marine nonjudicial punishment and insisted that he plead guilty at a special court-martial. This was of particular surprise to me as the convening authority knew my client not only professionally but socially as well. However, the government had a strong case, and my client agreed to plead guilty at a court-martial. He was fined, reduced a rank, and required to retire. However, the worst punishment was that he now had a criminal conviction that kept him from working in the field he had intended to work upon retiring from the Marine Corps.

I found out a couple of months later that the convening authority was being investigated for adultery himself. He eventually went to a board of inquiry and was retired at the next lower rank to the one that he had held. He did not receive a criminal conviction. Furthermore, he was engaging in adultery at the same time that he was giving my client a harsher-than-usual punishment for adultery. Although he would not admit it, it appears that he gave my client, who everyone knew that he liked, a relatively harsh punishment for adultery in hopes that it would make him look that he took a hard stand against adultery in order to cover up his own adultery.

Lastly, the convening authority can have a nonofficial interest in the case because he may feel that how he handles the case will affect his potential career advancement. This sometimes results in the convening authority referring charges for political reasons. It is true that people are sometimes charged for political reasons in the civilian sector as well, but the problem tends to be worse in the military.

Many convening authorities are very concerned with earning further promotions. They are senior officers who have invested a lot of time in the military, and they want to get the most out of it that they can. In and of itself, that is not necessarily wrong. Unfortunately, in the military justice arena, it can have drastic consequences. I have had multiple convening authorities tell me that they would rather refer any case that they think is close to trial and let the members panel do what they feel is just with the case rather than make the difficult decision not to send a case to trial. This especially occurs in rape cases where it is one person's word against another.* The evidence will not support the alleged victim's story, and yet the convening authority will send the case to trial anyway, even though the convening authority will agree that there is no realistic chance that the service member will be convicted. Forcing a service member to stand trial for a rape that he did not commit when there is not enough evidence to send the case to trial is a travesty of justice. It places the service member through a difficult ordeal, especially since the maximum punishment for rape is life without parole. The strain of facing spending the rest of your life in jail for a crime that you did not commit, even if that outcome is unlikely, is tremendous. There is also a substantial stigma attached with being tried for rape. Even if the service member is acquitted, his reputation will be tarnished for life.

> *Often referred to as "he-said-she-said cases" although I have seen a significant number of male-on-male sexual abuse cases.

One of my first clients was a senior enlisted member charged with rape. The so-called victim alleged that the rape occurred off base, so both the military and the civilian district attorney had jurisdiction in the case. The district attorney investigated the case and determined that there was insufficient evidence to send the case to trial. Almost two years after the allegation was first made, the Marine Corps decided to get involved. With no further evidence than the district attorney had, the Marine was sent to a general court-martial.

As I was not very experienced at the time, he chose to hire a civilian defense counsel, which is always a good choice when the military defense counsel does not have a lot of experience. The Marine was in fact acquitted of rape, but I saw firsthand the pressure and even agony that facing the life sentence placed not only on him but on his family as well. He also had to pay for his civilian attorney, and his reputation was destroyed.

Unfortunately, as I was to learn, such cases are not unusual. Some convening authorities believe that they will face little, if any, criticism, other than from the defense community, for sending a case to trial, despite the fact that it has very little evidence. On the other hand, the victim and victims' right organizations can be very upset over such decisions, and unlike the voices of the defense community, their voices can have sway with other more senior officers and even senators, which are required to approve promotion to the more senior ranks. To avoid the prospect of answering what they believe are difficult questions on why they did not send a case to trial, they simply send it to trial.

The Uniform Code of Military Justice does provide for a case being dismissed by the military judge if the convening authority has a personal interest in the case, and I would argue that all three of the above nonofficial interests are in fact personal interests.* Unfortunately, military judges require the defense to present proof, not just an inference, and the convening authority will almost always claim that he has nothing but a professional interest in the case whether or not it is true. I have only ever seen a military judge rule that a convening authority has a personal interest in the case when the convening authority was a victim of the alleged crime. Even in the case with the drowned drill instructor, where the investigating officer said that it was the command and the convening authority's fault that the Marine died and not my client's, the military judge ruled that the convening authority did not have a personal interest in the case. As a result, the law does very little to protect against injustices that occur when the convening authority has nonofficial interests in the case, and as long as commanding officers are convening authority, there will be a significant number of cases in which the convening authority has a nonofficial interest in the case.

> *If the case is in fact dismissed, it will generally be dismissed without prejudice, and a senior convening authority to the one that originally referred it will be allowed to refer the case to trial if he so chooses.

Because commanding officers are generally not attorneys, because they often know the accused, and because they can often have nonofficial interests in the outcome of a case, they should not act as a convening authority. The power to send a service member to a court-martial must be vested somewhere else to ensure justice.

The Convening Authority
Picks the Members

Another area that frequently causes injustice is in the selection of the members, the military equivalent of a jury. The convening authority selects the members panel, the same convening authority that decided whether or not to charge the case and what charges to bring. This is the equivalent of allowing the district attorney to select the jury in a civilian trial. It truly is an outrageous practice, but it has been allowed to continue in the military.

The practice is especially egregious because unlike in the civilian justice systems where a large pool is appointed (randomly) and then a select few are chosen from the jury pool to serve as the jury, in the military, all the members appointed serve on the court-martial unless they are excused. So instead of picking twelve jurors out of dozens of citizens, as is the case in the civilian justice systems, in the military, a typical members panel will be something along the lines of seven service members serving as members out of ten appointed for a general court-martial.* Because the members panel is so small and most service members appointed to a panel actually serve on the panel, it is much easier to appoint a panel in an attempt to get a specific result (often referred to as *stacking the panel*). A much higher percentage of people appointed actually serve because civilian courts generally have much lower standards for challenging a potential juror for cause than the military does. Also, most civilian jurisdictions have multiple peremptory challenges (which allow counsel to excuse a potential member or juror for any reason the counsel wishes to excuse him for, except that he may not be excused on the basis of race or gender) per side; whereas, the military has only one peremptory challenge per side. Simply appointing a couple of service members with the intent to ensure a specific result is often sufficient, especially if only a total of six are appointed (which is not unusual in a special court-martial) or even if ten are appointed (which is a common number appointed for a general court-martial). Since only three (special court-martial) or five (general court-martial noncapital—capital cases are very rare) members are required on a panel, I have seen several cases with as few as five or seven service members appointed, and technically, the convening authority can only appoint three or five. However, since there are usually a couple of members excused, the convening authority will rarely appoint a panel that does not include at least a couple of extra members. If the panel drops below the required amount, called *breaking quorum*, then the convening authority must appoint a new panel. Since appointing a new panel generally will make the trial start a day or so later, most convening authorities try to avoid having a quorum broken, and in fact, it is not very common for a quorum to be broken. Almost all courts-martial have witnesses that are flown in from out of the area, which is caused by the frequent rotation of service members, and every day that out-of-area witnesses are held at a court-martial, the convening authority's command has to pay for their food and lodging. So to keep costs down, convening authorities generally want to keep trials as short as possible. Obviously, the more service members that are appointed with the intent to receive a specific result, the more likely it is that the specific result sought will be achieved.

> *Only three members are required for a special court-martial, and only five are required for a general court-martial, unless the case is tried capitally, in which case twelve are required. These abnormally small panel requirements are the subject of the chapter "Small Members Panels."

There are two different ways that the convening authority attempt to influence the outcome of the court-martial through the appointing of the members panel. The first is a passive way to attempt to gain a certain result, and the second is an active way.

The passive way, and unfortunately a legal way, that the convening authority can attempt to control the outcome of a case is to place members on a panel that he believes will produce a certain result. This is accomplished through placing individuals of the panel that the convening authority believes have a particular view of criminal justice or of a particular crime. Since convening authorities often place members that they personally know on the panel, this is not really difficult. If you have worked with someone for a while in the military, you know whether they tend to be a pro-authority, law-and-order type of person, especially if you are on the lookout for service members that you want on a members panel. All it takes is a casual conversation about a criminal case that is in the news at the time to figure out an individual's general disposition toward alleged crimes is. Even if the convening authority is picking members that he does not personally know, he can easily ask the service member's immediate supervisor, and they can usually tell the convening authority about the potential member. Generally, convening authorities pick members that are more likely to convict and give harsher sentences since usually if the convening authority did not want the service member to be convicted, he would not have sent him to a court-marital. There are times, however, when a convening authority may send a service member to a court-martial but not actually want him to be convicted, for instance, if the convening authority knows and likes the accused or if the convening authority simply referred the case to trial for political reasons. This is fairly rare, but I have seen several cases where the members panel was unexpectedly prodefense or gave an exceptionally lenient sentence and the trial counsel believed that the convening authority had stacked the panel against him intentionally, and in a couple of those cases I tended to agree.

A convening authority also has the option of repeatedly detailing the same members to courts-martial. If the convening authority appoints a panel in one case and he likes the result from that case, the convening authority is free to appoint the exact same panel again or to reappoint many of the same members from the first court-martial. Most, but not all, military judges do help discourage this. Often they will grant a challenge for cause against a member that has recently served on multiple courts-martial. Almost all military judges will grant a challenge for cause against a member (remove that member from the panel) that has recently served on a similar case. Most military judges, however, do not grant challenges for cause as frequently as civilian judges despite the military appellate courts' instruction that military judges liberally grant challenges for cause. Part of the reason that many military judges are more reluctant to excuse members than most civilian judges could be because most civilian courts have a set number of jurors, usually twelve, and they will have a pool of potential jurors to get that twelve from that is several times larger than the required amount. So if the civilian judge excuses a juror, it simply rotates the next potential juror from the pool into the jury. Courts-martial do not have a set number of members, and all who are appointed serve unless they are excused. Military judges generally do not like to break quorum since it makes the trial take longer and that could explain, at least in part, why they are less likely to grant challenges. When the military judge is not interested in granting the challenge, he will rehabilitate the member—that is, cure the member's answer that left him open to the challenge, in this case that he had recently served on other courts-martial. The military judge can do this in two different easy ways. First, he can tell the member that he will instruct the panel that they may not consider anything from previous cases in any way in this case. The military judge will then ask the member if he will be able to follow that order. Of course, the response is always "Yes, sir." In reality, even if the member genuinely attempts to follow the military judge's instruction, human nature makes it practically impossible to ignore something that we know or have experienced. Another way that the military judge can rehabilitate the member is to ask the member if there is anything from the previous court-martial that would affect how the member would view this court-martial.* Again, despite human nature, the answer is almost always "No, sir." Based on the member's answers, the military judge then finds that there is no reason to exclude the member.

> *I've always wondered how the member is supposed to know the answer to that before he has actually heard the current court-martial.

Convening authorities do not always pick members with a particular result in mind, and I am sure that some convening authorities may never do it. But the potential is there, and no one but the convening authority would ever know about it, especially since most Marines by their very nature are progovernment anyway. Even if it was known that the convening authority picked members hoping for a certain result, there is nothing inherently illegal under the Uniform Code of Military Justice with putting progovernment members on a panel.

A convening authority can also actively attempt to control the outcome of a case through the appointing of members. This is an example of unlawful command influence and it is not allowed. The convening authority can actively attempt to control the outcome of the court-martial by telling a member or members that he wants a particular result in the case. The convening authority can do this directly by straight-out telling a member or members that he expects a specific result and by threatening their careers if they do not comply. The convening authority can do it indirectly, for example, by giving a speech to his officers on military justice in general and saying what he generally expects without mentioning the specific case.

Lastly, the convening authority is the commanding officer of the members, and he is often one of the officers that write their fitness reports. Fitness reports are generally written by the first officer up the chain of command from the service member receiving the fitness report and by that officer's immediate supervisor. For the more senior officers under the commanding officer, and some of the most senior enlisted on his staff, he will be that first officer (called a *reporting senior*) on the fitness report. For a substantial number of officers and a significant number of senior enlisted personnel, he will be the second officer (called the *reviewing officer*) on the fitness report.

The fact that the convening authority is the commanding officer of the members is always a problem because members are told as part of the court-martial that the case was referred to trial by the convening authority, their commanding officer. The temptation is always there to convict the accused because, after all, if the commanding officer did not want him convicted, he would not have sent him to a court-martial. The problem is further compounded by the fact that the members are also told that the convening authority, their commanding officer, appointed them as members as well. So in many instances, members know the convening authority—who writes their fitness report—sent the accused to trial and picked them to be a member. The temptation to convict simply to try to curry favor with the convening authority can be a strong one, and it is one that must be removed if justice is to prevail.

The convening authority should not be allowed to pick the members at a court-martial. It would shock most American's conscience to suggest that a civilian prosecutor should be allowed to pick the jury, yet in the military, those serve our country and protect freedom are subjected to allowing the person with the most civilian prosecutorial power pick their members panel. Our system of government tends to be built of checks and balances and the distribution of power; this system flies in the face of both. As the system exists, it is too easy to even legally influence the outcome of a trial, and there is too much temptation and too little oversight to prevent illegally influencing the outcome of a trial.

The Convening Authority's Power to Grant Witnesses and Consultants

Another area that engenders injustices is in the way witnesses and consultants are approved. The convening authority is also the approving authority for granting witnesses, expert or factual, and consultants. The same convening authority that decides to refer the charges, appoints the members panel, and is the commanding officer of the accused.

The law allows the convening authority to approve or disapprove witnesses because he provides the funds for witness's expenses from his command. If the witness is outside the local area, he will have to be flown in for the trial, lodged, and given money for food. In an expensive area like San Diego, where I tried most of my courts-martial, it can cost the government over one thousand dollars per witness for a weeklong trial, even more if the trial takes longer. Needless to say, most convening authorities are not willing to foot large bills for defense witnesses for someone that they already think is guilty since they referred the case to trial. So if the trial counsel has ten out-of-area witnesses that he wants, the convening authority is generally going to grant as few defense witnesses as possible since he is already looking at a ten-thousand-dollars-plus bill. And that is just for lay witnesses. Expert witnesses charge fees to consult and testify, and those fees are usually several hundred dollars an hour. An expert witness can easily cost the command over ten thousand dollars all by himself. A single expert for some cases can cost over a hundred thousand dollars.

Convening authorities personally exercise the power to grant or deny expert witnesses in most cases due to the cost of the experts. The convening authority normally delegates the authority to grant or deny factual witnesses to the trial counsel. If the defense wants a witness, they have to request him of the government, along with a proffer of what the witness will testify to. The government, either the convening authority directly or the trial counsel on the convening authority's behalf decides whether or not to grant the witness. If the witness is denied, the defense can then file a motion requesting that the military judge order the witness produced. Technically, the military judge cannot order the command to produce the witness or to do anything else, but he can order that the case be dismissed unless the government produces the witness. In fact, I had several cases where the convening authority refused to produce witnesses and the military judge had to abate, that is, cease proceedings, in the cases.

In almost all of the cases that I took to trial, I had to file a motion or even multiple sets of motions requesting that the military judge grant defense witnesses. Usually, I was able to get the military judge to grant me most, if not all, of the witnesses that the government had denied. This is an unnecessary and harmful step for most trials as defense witnesses are routinely denied by the convening authority or trial counsel because it takes no effort on their part to do so. They hope that the defense will not go through the effort of filing the motions to compel the production of witnesses or that the military judge will not rule for the defense on the motion. This wastes time, and if the accused has a civilian attorney, it can cost him significantly more money. Also, unfortunately, because it is an issue of cost to the command, some defense counsel are reluctant to fight the convening authority on witness issues because it can potentially be detrimental to their career. The injustices of timid and complicit defense counsel are catastrophic to an accused and are discussed in chapters titled "Inexperienced and Incompetent Judge Advocates" and "Government Control of Defense Counsel."

Whereas there are injustices in the approving of lay witness, it is in the area of expert consultants and witnesses that injustices truly abound. If the defense needs an expert, either as a consultant or a witness, he must ask the convening authority for the expert. Experts are very expensive and are often required in cases that have any evidence of a technical or scientific nature. Experts cover a wide range of topics, from DNA to pathology to ballistics, and so on.

Whenever the case has any scientific or technical evidence, usually the attorneys for each party will consult with an expert about what the evidence means or could mean and whether there is additional evidence that could be gathered. The injustice arises when the defense makes its request for an expert to the convening authority, and that it must justify its reason for requesting one. And if the convening authority denies the expert and the defense wishes to bring a motion requesting the court to order the expert, the defense must explain to the military judge why the expert is necessary.*

> *Again, although it is usually referred to as requesting the court to order the production of the expert and sometimes the court even says that it is ordering the production of the witness, the court cannot order the convening authority to produce the witness. All that the court can do is place the case in abeyance, that is, place

it on hold indefinitely until the convening authority complies, or the court can dismiss the case. The judge has no contempt power over the convening authority and generally cannot make him do anything. Of course, anytime the convening authority does not comply with the court, the military judge can dismiss the case, though military judges are usually very hesitant to do so for fear that they could be letting a guilty service member escape trial.

This is a terrible position for the defense to be in. In order to get an expert, they must tell the government what they plan to use him for. The government is made aware of what the defense intends to learn or offer through the expert, and they can adjust their trial strategy accordingly. Sometimes, the defense makes a tactical decision not to get an expert because that is better than telling the government what the defense is trying to do with the technical or scientific evidence.

For instance, if there is technical or scientific evidence in a case that has not been fully examined by the government, the defense will often not ask for an expert. As soon as they ask for an expert, the defense is letting the government know that they believe that there may be something important about that evidence. As such, the government may now go out and get an expert themselves when they had originally not planned to use an expert. This can be particularly damaging when the defense is not sure if an expert examination of the evidence will lead to conclusions that are favorable to the defense or that are favorable to the government. As a result, there are cases with evidence that would help the defense if it was properly examined by an expert, but it is never examined because the defense is afraid that if it asks for an expert and tells the government what it needs the expert to examine and why it needs the expert to examine it, the government will now consult an expert that they would not have otherwise consulted with and the examination of the evidence by the experts will lead to nothing favorable to the defense and to things that are favorable to the government which will then be presented against the accused at trial.

The only way that the defense can get an expert without telling the government why it needs the expert is if the accused pays for the expert himself. This is often very expensive, and many service members are unable to afford experts, especially if they have already had to pay for a civilian attorney.

The only way to avoid these injustices is to have witnesses and funds for experts approved by someone that is not interested in the outcome of the case. As long as the service member's commanding officer as the convening authority is making these determinations, there will be injustices, even with the judicial review. Furthermore, the defense must be allowed to obtain the services of experts without presenting their reasoning for using of the expert to the government before trial in order for the defense to be on equal footing with the government.

The Convening Authority's Action

Another problem with the commanding officer being the convening authority is that he also is the officer that is entrusted with the power to grant clemency and the authority to approve the conviction. The military has an unusual system of justice in many ways, but perhaps the single most unusual aspect is that all convictions and sentences must be approved by a nonjudicial individual, the convening authority. In civilian justice systems, governors and parole boards have the authority to grant clemency, that is, to reduce the severity of the punishment awarded by the court or even to pardon the convicted, but none of them are required to approve or disapprove the entire case.

In the military, after the court-martial is completed and there is a finding of guilty to any charge, the court-martial then has to determine the appropriate sentence to award. Both sides are given the opportunity to present evidence on sentencing and to argue what they believe is an appropriate sentence. The court-martial, the members if it is a trial by members, or the military judge, if it is a trial by military judge alone, will then award the sentence.

After the sentence is pronounced, the case is sent to the same convening authority who referred the case to trial. He is then required to approve or disapprove the results of the court-martial. This is called the *convening authority's action*.

Before the convening authority acts on the case, the defense has the opportunity to submit matters to the convening authority, called *clemency*, requesting that the convening authority lessen the punishment awarded by the court-martial or even disapprove of some or all the charges that the accused was convicted of.*

> *The convening authority can never change a finding of not guilty to a finding of guilty, and he can never award a harsher sentence that was awarded by the court-martial.

Some convening authorities grant clemency only very rarely; some grant clemency on a somewhat regular basis. I have never personally seen a convening authority disapprove a finding of guilty on even a single charge, let alone on all charges. Obviously, since the convening authority decided that the charge should be referred to the court-martial, the convening authority is unlikely to change his mind after the court-martial convicted the accused of the charge and disapprove the finding of guilty for the charge.

Having a process to grant clemency is a good thing, and the military should have a process to grant clemency. However, as long as the individual who referred the case to trial is the individual wielding that power, it will never be properly used to its full potential. Imagine a state civilian justice system vesting the power to grant clemency in the district attorney. It simply is a bad idea. The power to grant clemency will never be used to its fullest and intended purpose of promoting justice and equality in sentencing until it is taken away from the officer who referred the case to trial and given to a neutral officer, just as it is in the civilian justice system.

The Convening Authority Administratively Handling Serious Offenders

Injustices truly do happen at both ends of the spectrum. It is just as much an injustice for a man to receive too lenient a punishment as it is for a man to receive too harsh a punishment. A very important part of justice is balance. It is very easy for a justice system to create injustices on either end of the spectrum. Generally, the military justice system tends to create injustice by acting too harshly or not fairly enough toward the accused. However, one area where a fair amount of abuse occurs on the other end of the spectrum is in the administrative areas of nonjudicial punishment, summary courts-martial, and administrative separation boards.

Commanding officers are given the power under article 15 of the Uniform Code of Military Justice to punish minor offenders through a process called *nonjudicial punishment*, or *captain's mast*. The punishment that the commanding officer can give is relatively minor, and it depends on the rank of the officer imposing the nonjudicial punishment and on the rank of the individual receiving the nonjudicial punishment. The most serious punishments that can be given are forfeiture of one-half pay for two months, CCU (correctional custody unit) for thirty days or restriction for sixty days, and reduction of one rank. Also of note, there are many junior officers who are not convening authorities that have the power to impose nonjudicial punishment as well.

Nonjudicial punishment is designed to quickly and cheaply punish minor offenders. It is not a criminal proceeding, and a nonjudicial punishment conviction is not a criminal conviction. Usually the officer holding the nonjudicial punishment will hold it very shortly after he decides to impose it, often that same week. Nonjudicial punishment is a great tool for keeping order and discipline in the armed forces. There are a significant number of criminal offenses that are minor and unique to the military, such as being disrespectful, being late, or disobeying an order. These are unique military offenses, and handling them by a unique military procedure is appropriate and even desirable.

Another administrative measure available is a summary court-martial. A summary court-martial is somewhat of a misnomer since it is not a true court-martial. It is still an administrative and not a criminal measure. The punishment that can be given at summary court-martial is still fairly minor, but it is harsher than the punishment that can be given at nonjudicial punishment. The single most severe punishment that can be given is thirty years of confinement, and that can only be given to junior service members.

The service member can also simply be processed for administrative separation. This may be done alone or, as is usually the case, in conjunction with a summary court-martial or nonjudicial punishment. If a service member is administratively separated, he can be discharged with an honorable discharge, a general discharge, or an other-than-honorable discharge.

These administrative measures are a great benefit to the military. They allow minor offenses to be quickly and inexpensively handled. However, sometimes the system is abused. Most nonmilitary specific crimes should be handled at a criminal, not administrative, level. Some nonmilitary specific crimes are appropriately handled at nonjudicial punishment like minor assaults or drug use.* However, by and large, most nonmilitary-specific crimes should be handled at the appropriate level of court-martial. Unfortunately, sometimes very serious charges are handled at administrative levels. Crimes ranging from sexual assaults to drug distribution are sometimes handled administratively. This is relatively rare, but when it does happen, it is a serious injustice.

> *If a service member uses an illegal drug, he is required to be processed for administrative separation, although he is not required to be separated, and often is not if it is his first offense and he has otherwise been a good service member. Because there is already an additional procedure that is in place, nonjudicial punishment is a good forum to handle many drug-use cases. It is much quicker and cheaper than a court-martial.

Administratively handling a serious offender, and thus giving the offender only minor punishment, has an adverse impact on our justice system and on the victim of the crime. It causes victims to not only lose faith in our justice system but also in the military leaders that failed to ensure justice was accomplished. This leads to a longer healing process for the victim, distrust of the government, and even potential vigilante action by that victim or by other victims who fear that the same thing will happen in their case.

Administratively handling serious offenders also breaks down the deterrent effect of the justice system. Ideally, men should do right out of a love from their Creator, and if not for their love of God, at least out of love or respect for their fellow men. However, there are many people who simply refrain from committing crimes because of the fear for the punishment if they are caught. And, unfortunately, the military has many such individuals in it. If the perceived benefit for doing the wrong outweighs the perceived risk and punishment of being caught, these individuals will commit the crime. Administratively handling serious offenders is the exact kind of government behavior that can encourage these people to break the law.

Many serious offenders are also a danger to society. These individuals need to be identified and processed by the criminal justice system, and not handled administratively. Some people simply need to spend time incarcerated. First, while they are incarcerated, they are not a threat to society at large. Secondly, while they are incarcerated, they can be sent to rehabilitation programs. After having spent years as a criminal defense attorney, I am skeptical of most rehabilitation programs for most offenders. However, sending people to a rehabilitation program with a low success rate is better than not doing anything at all.

Lastly, justice requires that people be punished for wrongdoing. Government is to encourage right actions and punish wrong actions. By failing to appropriately punish individuals from criminal behavior, government is abdicating one of its most basic responsibilities, and injustice flourishes.

Administrative measures are great and proper tool of military justice. However, it is destructive to justice when they are used for crimes that they are not suited for.

The Convening Authority Having Other Responsibilities

A commanding officer is a very important person in the military, and he has many great responsibilities. Many commanding officers spend very long hours fulfilling their duties. Handling military justice issues is just one responsibility, and not even the most important one, on most commanding officer's list of tasks.

A commanding officer is responsible for all that his unit does or fails to do. He will have anywhere from hundreds to tens of thousands of service members under him. He is responsible not only for the mission of the unit, but also for ensuring that the unit upholds required individual and unit standards. All missions are important, but the missions of combat units are especially important.

The armed services chose this very busy individual and gave him one more great responsibility, to be the convening authority of his unit. There are not very many responsibilities that take priority of over criminal justice matters, but the Armed Forces managed to find someone that had other greater responsibilities and made him the convening authority for very important military justice matters. A few dozen courts-martial, even if some of them include the possibility of someone being sentenced to life without the possibility of parole, or even death, do not seem as important when the convening authority's other responsibility is to be a commanding officer in a time of war and literally have the lives of tens of thousands of Americans and even the United States war effort in his hands.

Those service members accused of crimes, and those victims of crimes, deserve to have someone responsible for the military justice system that focuses solely on military justice. Too much is at stake to have military justice handled by someone that has other greater responsibilities. People's lives are literally at stake. Life-and-death decisions must be made. The military almost never executes service members, but life sentences are not uncommon. If a service member is wrongfully confined, he can never recover those wasted years. If a violent offender is allowed to remain in society and harms other people, those people or their families cannot undo the harm that they suffer. Civilians are afforded a district attorney whose sole focus and responsibility is criminal justice. The military deserves no less.

The Solution to the Convening Authority Injustices

There are many serious problems that plague the military justice system through the convening authority. Many of these are simply fixed through taking the convening authority's power away from commanding officers and giving it to a judge advocate. This billet does not exist, so there is no name for it. The name is not what is important anyway, but for the sake of ease, I will give it one: the *referral authority*. The referral authority should be a senior judge advocate that passes through a screening process to get the billet, just as military judges have a screening process that determines whether they are fit to be judges. Referral authorities could be appointed either for geographic locations (i.e., a base or bases) or for units (i.e., all members of a division-sized unit have the same Referral authority regardless of where they are stationed). The referral authority should be given the authority to convene and refer cases to both general courts-martial and special courts-martial. The commanding officer should still retain the power to conduct administrative measures such as nonjudicial punishment and summary courts-martial. The commanding officer and his attorney, the staff judge advocate, should certainly be able to share their concerns about whether or not to charge a service member with the referral authority, but the referral authority should be completely independent of the command and exercise his own judgment in whether to refer charges.

First and foremost, this would eliminate the problems caused by having a convening authority that is not an attorney. An attorney is best suited to make the decision of what cases to refer to trial. An attorney is less likely to refer cases that should not be referred and more likely to refer those that should. This is the exact reason that district attorneys and United States Attorneys are attorneys. The specialized training required to justly administer criminal law requires that it be handled by an attorney. In many ways, no single individual in any criminal justice system has more power than the individual who decides what individuals to prosecute and what charges to prosecute them with. The position that arguably has the most power certainly should not be the position with the least legal training, education, and experience. The district attorney concept has served the American civilian justice system very well, and it would do the same for the Armed Forces.

Secondly, by creating a referral authority, giving him the sole authority to refer cases to trial, the problems caused by having cases referred to trial by an officer who knows the accused would be eliminated. The convening authority is the commanding officer, and he knows many of the service members in his unit. A referral authority would be an attorney who would not actually work with service members in standard units. He would have his trial counsel and his support staff that worked for him, not an entire unit. This would help ensure the fair and impartial administration of justice. Furthermore, if the referral authority did in fact know a service member that was facing criminal charges, he should be required to forward the charges without comment to a different referral authority to determine the disposition of the charges.

Creating a referral authority instead of making the commanding officer the convening authority would also help eliminate service members being sent to courts-martial over improper nonofficial interests of the commanding officer. Such concerns can never be completely eliminated as whoever has the authority to charge service members may sometimes do so for the wrong reason. However, the temptation to improperly refer a case to trial to cover up failures or crimes by the command will be drastically reduced since the commanding officer will no longer be making the decision of whether to send a service member to trial.

Creating a referral authority would also create an officer with a more substantial level of professional independence, like a judge. This would help eliminate the problem of referring cases to trial simply because it is perceived as beneficial to the commanding officer's career to refer anything rather than making the difficult decision to determine that there is not enough evidence and the case should not go to trial.

The concepts of administrative punishments such as nonjudicial punishment and summary courts-martial are uniquely military. They have proved to be valuable tools in keeping good order and discipline in the armed services. They are a quick, easy, and inexpensive way to handle minor offenses. This helps keep the criminal justice system from being bogged down with the minor issues. Commanding officers should still be allowed to exercise these administrative measures. However, administrative measures should be restricted to purely military crimes, such as unauthorized absences, disobeying orders, and disrespect. If the offense was grievous enough, the referral authority should still have the authority to refer the case to trial. And as it currently is, a service member should have the option of refusing the administrative measure and assuming the risk of being court-martialed. Lastly, the referral authority should still be able to send cases that are not purely military offenses to the commanding officer for nonjudicial punishment or a summary court-martial if he felt that the crime was minor enough to be handled at that level and the service member consented to having the case handled at the level. This would help eliminate the injustices from thee chapter "The Convening Authority Administratively Handling Serious Offenders," that is, those which are caused by commanding officers imposing nonjudicial punishment or sending serious offenders to summary courts-martial. The other major administrative measure, administrative separation, should be left alone since it is technically supposed to be used to discharge service members that are no longer of value to the military, not punish service members for wrongdoing. The commanding officer should have the authority to discharge a service member administratively after the referral authority has handled the criminal aspect of the case if in the commanding officer's opinion the individual is no longer fit to serve and the service member was not given a punitive discharge by the court-martial. Administrative separation is also used to discharge service members that have not done anything criminally wrong but are not fit to serve. Examples of this are service members who are not technically proficient in their jobs or service members who do not meet the physical requirement of their service.

The concept of the referral authority, or *district attorney* as the position is called in the civilian world (United States Attorney on the federal civilian side), is the same one that has served our country well in the civilian world, and it should be employed in the military as well. This would help eliminate the injustices from chapters " The Convening Authority Refers Cases to Trial" and "The Convening Authority Having Other Responsibilities," which are that the commanding officer refers cases to trial and that the commanding officer has many other responsibilities other than military justice matters.

Taking away the role of the convening authority from the commanding officer and giving it to a referral authority fixes many of the injustices caused by the convening authority, but it does not fix all of them. Part of the problem is that the military justice system vests too much authority in one individual. The American system of government rests upon the principle that power must be divided between multiple branches and levels of government. That same principle should apply to military justice as well. Just as the commanding officer should not have the power to grant or deny defense witness and consultant requests, the referral authority should not exercise that power either. The injustices arise when the same individual who has the authority to send a case to trial has the authority to deny the defense witnesses and consultants that it needs to properly defend the case.

The government has a friendly ear when they request witnesses and consultants since that request is made to the commanding officer as the convening authority.* One effective way to correct the injustices would be to allow the commanding officer to continue to grant witnesses and consultants for the government and allow the regional defense counsel to grant witnesses and consultants for the defense. That would ensure that the defense is at least theoretically on equal footing with the government in securing witnesses and consultants. Furthermore, the defense would no longer have to disclose prematurely to the government that they were seeking an expert. Obviously, the defense would still have to disclose to the government before trial if they intended to use an expert witness. The funding for the defense witnesses and consultants could either come from the command as it currently does, or headquarters could provide funds directly to the regional defense counsel to use to fund the witnesses and consultants. Under this method, both the trial counsel and the defense counsel should generally be satisfied with the witnesses and consultants that they receive; however, both should be allowed to request the court to order the witnesses and consultants in the event that they believe that they were improperly denied. The military judge would have to be given the authority to order the commanding officer or the regional defense counsel to grant the witnesses and consultants.** In the event that the commanding officer or regional defense counsel did not comply with the judge's order, he would have to be granted the authority to order them confined for contempt of court. The court would still have to have the power to review the regional defense counsel's decisions in the event that he and the defense counsel disagree. That is to ensure that the accused is not being denied his right to compel witnesses, although such requests for judicial review should be rare. The military judge would have to have the authority to review the commanding officer's decisions as well to ensure that a commanding officer who disagrees with the referral authority's decision to send a case to trial does not defeat the ability of the government to try the case by refusing to fund any witnesses for the case. This would correct the injustices of the chapter "The Convening Authority's Power to Grant Witnesses and Consultants" since the commanding officer would no longer make determinations dealing with witnesses or consultants for the defense.

*In the *Manual for Courts-Martial*, the trial counsel is listed as the approving authority for witnesses. However, it is actually the commanding officer since he is the one that pays for them. If he refuses to pay for the witness, they are not coming, and it does not matter that the trial counsel has approved them. If the commanding officer does not grant the government's witnesses, the trial counsel has no recourse. However, since the commanding officer decided to charge the case, he will normally pay for a witness the trial counsel requests. Some commanding officers actually require the trial counsel to get approval from them; most however simply allow the trial counsel to handle both government and defense witness requests unless there is significant cost involved, such as in the case of expert witnesses and consultants.

**Currently, the military judge only has the authority to dismiss or stay the case.

Another power that the commanding officer exercises as the convening authority that the referral authority should not have is the power to appoint the members. The same abuses that are caused by allowing the convening authority to appoint the members would exist if the referral authority appointed the members. To avoid these injustices, the members should be randomly picked, just as they are in the civilian justice systems. The best way to do this and to ensure that it is done impartially would be to have the commanding officers forward to the clerk of the court all available service members in their command by rank.* The names would then be placed into a computer program that would randomly pick the appropriate number of members. The clerk would then call each prospective member and verify that they would be available for the dates of the trial (i.e., that they are not going to be on leave or out of the area on official business). In the event that the commanding officer feels that a particular service member is mission essential and cannot be away from his duties to serve as a member, he should have the ability to request that the military judge remove that person as a prospective member before the panel is actually formally assembled. If the military judge agreed and removed the member, then the clerk of court would randomly pick another member to take the place of the excused member. This would ensure that members were not being picked in an attempt to influence the outcome of the case and would correct the injustices of the chapter "The Convening Authority Picks the Members" since an impartial selection process would now be used to pick members.

*The members must be senior to the accused.

The last power that the commanding officer has as the convening authority that needs to be placed elsewhere is the authority to grant clemency and to approve or disapprove the conviction. First, the judgment of the court-martial should not have to be approved by anyone. Courts-martial are federal courts, and it is embarrassing that their results are considered so questionable as to require approval, especially by someone other than an attorney as the system currently stands. If the corrections suggested in this book were implemented, courts-martial would consistently produce just results, much the same as our civilian justice systems. Justice systems rest on humans, and humans can never eliminate all error or injustice; however, having the court-martial results approved does more harm than good. Injustices are very rarely corrected by this process, and it unnecessarily delays the case from being sent to the appellate courts. Thus, this arcane step should be eliminated. The case would still be reviewed by the appellate courts. This is the proper way to review a verdict, and it is the only way that the military should use.

The power to grant clemency should be vested solely in the parole board. This power is too great to be wielded by the individual who decided that the case should go to trial. If the power is given to a parole board, not only will a neutral party decide whether clemency is appropriate, but since all one body will rule on all requests, it will also help ensure uniformity and fairness in the administration of clemency. The military already has parole boards, and they alone should exercise this power.

In addition to clemency from the parole board, service members would still be free to petition the president for clemency or for a pardon. Many service members do request pardons or clemency from the president, and most presidents give pardon or clemency to multiple service members each year.

By taking the authority to convene courts-martial away from the commanding officer and creating a referral authority, picking members randomly by the court clerk, vesting authority to grant defense witnesses and consultants in the regional defense counsel, and giving clemency power to a parole board, the injustices caused by the current system would be drastically reduced. Although the injustices caused by the convening authority are the most prevalent and most severe, there are, unfortunately, other things that routinely cause injustices, and they are addressed in the following chapters.

MEMBERS INJUSTICES

In this section, injustices that are caused by the members panel itself are exposed. There are three of them: only two-thirds have to vote guilty in order to convict, the required number of service members on the panels is too small, and members often know witnesses and counsel. The way to correct each injustice is at the end of the chapter.

A Concurrence of Only Two-Thirds of the Members Renders a Verdict of Guilty

The first injustice caused by the members panel is that only two-thirds of the members have to vote guilty for a verdict of guilty. In most civilian justice systems, the verdict must be unanimous. If the jury cannot reach a unanimous decision, the judge declares a mistrial, and the government must decide whether they wish to retry the case. In the military, if less than two-thirds of the members vote for a finding of guilty, then the verdict of the members is not guilty. There are no hung members' panels for verdicts in the military.

There are advantages to having a system that gives a verdict each time and does not result in hung juries. That eliminates the need for spending more time and money on retrials. It also allows for more certainty and finality for defendants since they do not face the potential of enduring multiple trials. This is one of the few areas where the military justice system is actually better than most civilian justice systems. The entire procedure does not need to be discarded, but it does need to be modified. Two-thirds is simply too low a percentage. The system should be kept where any consensus by the members for a finding of guilty above a certain percentage results in a finding of guilty, and anything below that required percentage results in a finding of not guilty. However, the military should use four-fifths, not two-thirds. Only three members are required for a special court-martial and only five for a general court-martial. (This is a problem in and of itself and is addressed later.) That means that at a special court-martial with the minimum required number of members, only two people need to vote guilty for a guilty verdict. Out of nine at a general court-martial (and most general courts-martial have nine or fewer members), only six need to vote for a verdict of guilty. This is simply not enough protection against an unjust guilty verdict. If the government is really able to prove its case beyond a reasonable doubt, they should be able to get four-fifths of the members to agree. This still keeps a member who, for whatever reason, refuses to agree with the vast majority from wrongfully giving a verdict of not guilty or hanging the jury. If the size of the members panels are increased to a minimum of five for a special court-martial and ten for a general court-martial, as I recommended later in this book, then four members and eight members respectively would have to agree for a guilty verdict. This certainly does not place the government in an unduly difficult position, and it will help ensure that innocent service members are not convicted. As the system stands, a service member can potentially be convicted by only two members. That simply is not enough people. The rights of the accused are not adequately protected when so few can find him guilty.

If very few civilian justice systems are satisfied with less than a unanimous finding for a verdict of guilty, why should the Armed Forces accept a percentage as low as two-thirds for those who are serving our country? If the government actually has proof beyond a reasonable doubt that a service member is guilty, the government will be able to convince four-fifth to vote guilty. This would also still serve justice by protecting against a single member, or two members in larger panels, that simply refuse to render a guilty for whatever the reason, despite the evidence. A large component of any valid justice system is balancing the rights of the individual (that is, from being wrongfully convicted or punished) and the rights of society (that is, to have guilty people punished thus providing for public safety and justice). A four-fifths verdict is a good balance of both; two-thirds infringes on individual rights and risks innocent people being convicted.

Small Members Panels

Another serious injustice is the small members panels used in the military. Only three members are required for special courts-martial (the military misdemeanor equivalent court), and only five for general courts-martial (the military felony equivalent court). The only exception to this is for capital cases which require twelve members.

This is another area of injustice that is caused by the military deviating for the civilian justice systems. Most civilian justice systems require twelve jurors for felony trials and six for misdemeanor trials. If the military wants to potentially take away the freedom of a service member, they should be required to provide similar levels of personal rights that civilian systems provide to civilians. There is no justifiable unique military situation which would require the military to be allowed to use such substantially smaller members panels. If a command does not have enough personnel for the court-martial, they can use personnel from other units on the base, which is already done in cases that require it. Most bases have thousands or even tens of thousands of personnel stationed at them. It is not an undue burden to require the larger member panels. Furthermore, if there are not enough members on the base under the current system, then members are taken from other bases. The process would be exactly the same if the system was changed to require the larger member panels.

The reason larger numbers are required on the civilian systems and should be required in the military systems is to ensure that a fair cross section of society, or the military, is represented on the panel. There should be people from different walks of life with different views and experiences. This helps to ensure a fair members panel, one that is not unduly extreme, either in favor of the government or in favor of the accused.

The military should be required to have at least ten members for a general court-martial and at least five for a special court-martial. This would alleviate the injustices caused by having so few people decide the fate of an accused.

Members Knowing Witnesses or Counsel

The last source of members panel injustices is one that tends to plague smaller units and bases more. That injustice is that some of the members often know one or more of the witnesses or counsel in the trial. While on active duty, I tried about half my cases at the Marine Corps Recruit Depot–San Diego. This base was also responsible for the Western Recruiting Region (all Marine Corps recruiting west of the Mississippi). MCRD–San Diego is one of the smaller Marine bases. It was unusual that I tried a case or saw a case tried in which there were no members that knew either witnesses or counsel. Often most of the panel knew counsel for both sides, and several different members knew several different witnesses. This problem was not as frequent on the larger Marine bases or Navy bases where I tried cases, but it did occasionally occur at larger bases as well.

The simple and logical solution to having a member that knows a witness or counsel is to excuse that member. The members are asked during voir dire if they know any of the witnesses or counsel on the case.* Many counsel will challenge a member that knows a witness or the opposing counsel unless the member barely knows the individual. Unfortunately, many military judges do not grant challenges against members unless they know the witness or counsel very well. This applies to challenges for cause, that is, counsel asking the court to remove a member for a specific reason allowed by law. If the member knows a witness, he may not be able to impartially judge what the individual testifies to. If the member knows one of the attorneys, he may not be able to impartially weigh his arguments. Attorneys are afforded an unlimited number of challenges for cause.** If the court does not grant the challenge, then counsel may still use a peremptory challenge and excuse a member simply because the counsel wants to. However, counsel are only afforded one peremptory challenge.

> *Voir dire is the questioning of members by court and counsel before they are seated to determine if there are any reasons to challenge a member. If a challenge to a member is granted by the military judge, that member will not serve on the members panel.

> **The only exception to this is that it cannot be exercised because of the member's race or gender.

What often happens when a member answers that he knows a witness or counsel is that either the opposing counsel, if he wants the member, or the military judge will rehabilitate the member. This is done by determining if the member's relationship with the witness or counsel will affect the member's ability to be fair and impartial. This is done by questioning the member about how he knows the witness or counsel, when he met him, and how much interaction he has with him. The member is then asked if he feels that he can fairly and impartially evaluate the testimony (if it is a witness that he knows) or arguments (if it is a counsel that he knows) of the individual and properly weigh the testimony or arguments without giving them more or less weight simply because he knows them. The member almost always replies that he can.

Most members probably really believe that they can be fair and impartial despite the fact that they know someone; however, that is simply contrary to human nature. If you know someone and have a positive impression of them, you are much less likely to believe that they are lying or mistaken. Many military judges routinely deny challenges for cause when the member interacts with the witness or counsel several times a month. These military judges rule that because of the member's limited interaction with the witness and because of the member's statement that he will not give the testimony or argument of the person he knows undue weight, that the member will in fact be impartial. However, there are many Marines that I only interact with several times a month that I personally would not be able to impartially evaluate their testimony if they were a witness or their argument as a counsel. Most members simply do not appreciate what is at stake in a court-martial and human nature. Many people like to pride themselves on being impartial and will not admit that knowing someone will affect their judgment of them, but the truth is that, if a member knows someone, they will have an opinion of them, either good or bad. Members should be neutral at the start of the trial and have no opinion of any witnesses or counsel. There is no good reason to have members serve that know counsel or witness, and the risk of a member giving undue weight to someone they know is simply too great to allow when a service member's liberty and future are at stake. The law should require that members who know either a witness or an attorney on the case be excused from serving.

MILITARY JUDGE INJUSTICES

In this section, injustices caused by the military judge are addressed. There are two of them: First, the military judges do not have enough authority to properly administer justice, and second, some military judges lack the proper criminal experience to be a military judge. These injustices are easily corrected by giving the military judges the same level of authority that civilian federal judges have in criminal cases and by ensuring that only judge advocates with substantial criminal experience are chosen as military judges.

Military Judges Have Insufficient Power

One of the most powerful figures in American government is the federal judge. Federal civilian judges, be they district court judges (federal trial judges), court of appeals judges (intermediate appellate court judges), or Supreme Court justices (final appellate court judges) have the ability to issue orders and decisions that not only do the actual people in front of the court have to abide by, but others do as well, even other governmental entities, to include the president of the United States. Federal judges have contempt power which allows them to fine or even confine noncompliant individuals, even government officials. They can void acts by state and even federal legislatures, governors, the president, and even the acts of the people through referendums. Classical conservatives and states' rights advocates have, from the foundation of our nation, criticized the power of federal judges as abusive. For example, consider the following from Thomas Jefferson:

> It has long been my opinion, and I have never shrunk from its expression,...that the germ of dissolution of our Federal Government is in the constitution of the Federal Judiciary—an irresponsible body (for impeachment is scarcely a scare-crow), working like gravity by night and by day, gaining a little today and a little tomorrow, and advancing its noiseless step like a thief over the field of jurisdiction until all shall be usurped from the States and the government be consolidated into one. To this I am opposed. (Thomas Jefferson to Charles Hammond, 1821)

I agree that the federal judiciary exercises too much power. However, military judges are on the opposite end of the spectrum. They have too little power, and it results in their inability to properly dispense justice in certain cases. Justice, and government, requires balance. Whereas military judges do not need to be given the full amount of power that civilian federal judges have, they do need to be given the same power to preside over courts-martial that federal judges have in presiding over criminal trials. (Courts-martial are federal courts, and as such, military judges can be referred to as federal judges. However, common use is to refer to them as military judges and to refer to federal civilian judges as federal judges. In this book, only federal civilian judges are referred to by the title *federal judge*.)

Military judges have control over very little other than over the accused and counsel that are actually before them for a particular case. The military judge does not even have real control over the convening authority. If the military judge orders the convening authority (either in his capacity as the convening authority or in his capacity as the commanding officer) to do or refrain from doing something and he does not comply, all the military judge can do is abate the proceedings (place the case on indefinite hold) or order the case dismissed. Unfortunately, some military judges are often reluctant to take such drastic measures to enforce a court order. For instance, if a service member is charged with rape or murder, most judges rightfully want to see the individual tried and punished if he is found guilty. That makes them very reluctant to dismiss the case on a technicality or because the convening authority is not complying with a court order. Usually, these situations arise when the court requires the command to provide funding for defense witnesses, experts, or travel (to see the scene of the crime, interview witnesses, etc.). Most commands comply with the military judges, but because the convening authority often outranks the military judges* and because the convening authority is the one who convened (ordered) the court, some commanding officers resist following court orders that they disagree with. Military judges must be given the authority to enforce orders against commands and commanding officers through contempt proceedings. The current military contempt proceedings are weak and almost never used and then used only against individuals actually before the court (the counsel, the members, witnesses, or the accused). The military judges need the same power to hold individuals in contempt that civilian federal judges have. If the military judge can order an individual fined or imprisoned for disobeying a court order, even if the individual is not physically present in the court and regardless of the individual's rank, it will make people much more likely to fully comply with the court's orders. It also allows the court to punish the commanding officer for disregarding a court order rather than punishing the society at large by dismissing a case and allowing a potentially dangerous criminal to be released back into society without a trial.

> *A convening authority for a general court-martial is almost always a general or admiral and as such will outrank all military judges since their highest rank is colonel or captain.

Injustices can be caused by the commanding officer not complying with a court order, but the most common source of injustices comes from other governmental agencies not complying with a court order. The court truly has very little power over these agencies and the individuals that work for them since they often do not care if the military judge orders the case dismissed. Not only does the court lack power over these individuals, but the commanding officer usually does as well. The most common culprit in Southern California during my tour was Naval Medical Center Balboa. Balboa is responsible for the medical issues for most of the Marines and sailors stationed in the Southern California area. Balboa is also responsible for conducting mental evaluations for service members when ordered by the court or the command. When there is reason to suspect that the accused may not have been mentally responsible for his actions or may not be mentally competent to assist in his defense, rule 706 of the *Manual for Courts-Martial* requires that the accused be given a mental examination. This examination is called a *706 examination*. Ideally, these issues will be resolved early in the trial, but sometimes the commanding officer refuses to order the 706 examination* or the defense counsel does not raise it until after referral. Once the case has been referred to trial, the military judge generally wants to keep it on a pretty tight timeline. If the military judge orders a 706 examination, he will often direct that it be completed by a certain time in order to respect the accused's right to a speedy trial, to try to keep costs associated with delaying a case down, and to ensure the speedy administration of justice. Unfortunately, Balboa often ignores the timeline imposed by the military judge and completes the examination on their own time schedule and there really is not anything that the court can do about it. Balboa is also often the source of expert consultants or witnesses for medical issues. There can also be issues with providing the expert and doing so in a timely manner and consistent with the court's order.

> *Until the case is referred to trial, the commanding officer has the authority to order the 706.

Balboa is not the only culprit. Other governmental entities from time to time refuse to turn over evidence such as safety reports or various investigations or they take a long time to turn them over.

Civilian federal judges simply order the individual to comply with the court's order, and if they do not, the judge holds the culprit in contempt and can fine or even imprison the noncompliant individual. If military judges had the same power, it would be rare that other governmental entities would ignore their orders. Furthermore, once punished, most would immediately comply to avoid further punishment. Military judges must be given this same contempt authority that federal judges have to ensure that they can properly administer justice.

Military Judges with Little Criminal Experience

Another problem with military judges is that they often lack significant criminal, and sometimes even legal, experience. Whereas the military judges do not currently have the power as they should, they still play a very significant role in the military justice system. If they are given more of the power as civilian federal judges have, then they will have an even greater role. In the course of a trial, a military judge will often have to make hundreds of legal decisions. He will have to rule on motions, objections by counsel, ensure that the court is being properly and orderly run, and be on the lookout for anything improper that either attorney, the members, the witness, or anyone else is doing that is not being objected to by counsel, either because they have missed it or because they think, for whatever reason, that it is in the best interests of the side that they represent not to object. Some of these legal decisions the military judge will have time to research and think about, such as is in the case of written motions. But many of the legal decisions will be made with little time to reflect or research. Of course, the military judge can always adjourn the court and take time if he feels that he needs to, but usually that is a matter of last resort as most military judges tend to want to keep the trial moving. In order to properly make all these important legal decisions, it is important that the individual making them has the proper experience to make them. Unfortunately, many judge advocates are serving as military judges without the proper experience to accurately make these decisions.

This is a problem that is not unique to the military and is one of the few sources of military injustices that cannot be corrected by simply adapting the prevailing civilian practice. Civilian judges are either appointed or elected.* States either appoint or elect their judges. Elected judges present several problems. First there are always concerns that some of them are acting as politicians not judges. They may rule on high-profile cases in the way that they believe will make them most popular with the voting populace, not necessarily the way that the law would require them to rule. This is especially true in cases involving issues important to special interest groups. Another problem with elected judges is that it can result in the more charismatic attorneys, not necessarily the better attorneys, becoming the judges. People often do not understand what is required to be a good judge and they usually cannot even tell whether or not a candidate is a good attorney. This tends to make some people vote for the more likable candidate. Of course, many people that do take the time to vote do not take the time to research judges, and so they just vote for the one running under the party affiliation that they prefer. The final problem with elected judges is that, like others running for public office, they have to rely on campaign funds. Most elected judges get their campaign funds from two sources—special interest groups and other attorneys. Other people generally do not care enough about which judge gets elected to contribute money to an election campaign. Of course, this practice creates concerns that, whenever a special interest group or attorney that gave money to the judge's election campaign appears in the judge's court, the judge may not be impartial.

*Federal civilian judges are appointed by the president and confirmed by a majority vote in the Senate.

The practice of appointing judges is not without criticism either. Generally appointed judges are appointed by the governor. There is always the feeling that some appointed judges are appointed to make sure that the political agenda of the one appointing them is carried out or that they are being appointed to repay political favors and may not be the most qualified individuals for the position.

Different states have different requirements for someone to be appointed or to be elected as a judge. It also usually depends on which court the judge will be in. Judges in magistrate courts, misdemeanor courts in some states, or family courts will generally have less requirements that a judge on an appellate level court. Requirements can range from very lax to very stringent.

In the military, judges are assigned, but not by a politician. A judicial screening board examines potential military judges. If a judge advocate is selected, and the manpower element of the particular services headquarters approves the assignment, he will be sent to a special class for military judges. If he passes, he will then be assigned to be a judge for a particular circuit.

The concept of a judicial screening board is a good one. It is the best way, in a military setting, to obtain the most qualified military judges. Ideally, it does away with the problems of having a politician appoint judges and with the problems of having the judges elected. However, military judges are routinely being selected by that lack of the required experience.

There are several factors that tend to contribute to unqualified military judges being selected. The first issue tends to be unique to the Marine Corps. In the Marine Corps, there are a significant number of senior officers serving as judge advocates that have only been judge advocates for short periods of time. There are two different programs in place in the Marine Corps that send currently serving officers to law school. When these officers graduate from law school, they are generally majors (O-4) or will be promoted to major very shortly. Because of their relative seniority, they are placed in important billets, even though they have no legal experience. From those billets, they are then selected to be military judges, even though at this point they still only have a few years of legal experience. Some of them not only have little experience as an attorney, but even worse have almost no experience in military criminal law. Some of these judge advocates are being selected to be military judges even though they have never tried a single contested case as lead counsel.

The military needs to set minimum requirements in order to even be considered to serve as a military judge. At a minimum to be considered for such an important position, a judge advocate should have served six years* as a judge advocate. He should also have spent at least four years practicing criminal law and at least one year as both a defense counsel and a trial counsel. This would ensure that more seasoned and experienced attorneys become military judges. Most candidates should have significantly more experience than the minimum.

*Generally two full tours.

If the military is unable to keep enough judge advocates with the requisite skill and experience to be military judges, then the military needs to give increased bonuses to judge advocates as an incentive for them to continue to serve. While I served, the Marine Corps had the smallest bonuses at the time—a one-time thirty-thousand-dollar bonus over a three-year period for agreeing to stay in for an extra three years after serving the initial required time. That bonus may be going away as well. (The other branches offer much higher bonuses. As such, they have higher retention among their judge advocates. This leads to a larger, more experienced pool from which to choose military judges, which is why other branches do not have as much of a problem with inexperienced military judges.) By comparison, many medical doctors are eligible for yearly bonuses much larger than that thirty thousand. Most Marine judge advocates do not stay in long enough to be promoted to major, the rank that is required to be a military judge. Officers usually serve ten years in the Marine Corps before they are promoted to major.

Ensuring that the military keeps more senior judge advocates and appoints only those with significant experience to be military judges will go a long way to reduce the current injustices in our system. It would also save the government significant time and money in the long run as fewer mistakes would be made. Mistakes can be very expensive to fix in the legal system.

COUNSEL INJUSTICES

This section addresses injustices that are caused by the counsel, both trial and defense, that are actually serving on the cases. These injustices are that the trial counsel has subpoena authority and the defense counsel does not, the inexperience of many trial counsel and defense counsel, and the command and/or staff judge advocate control of some defense counsel.

Unequal Subpoena Power

Another injustice is that trial counsel have the authority to issue subpoenas, and defense counsel do not. If there is evidence that the trial counsel believes is relevant to the case, he can issue a subpoena requiring whoever has the evidence to produce it. In most cases, he does not have to obtain permission or notify anyone that he is issuing a subpoena.* The results of the subpoena are discoverable so if the defense counsel has submitted a discovery request, he will receive the evidence that the trial counsel obtains as well. Also if the evidence is exculpatory—that is, it tends to show that the accused may be not guilty—the trial counsel has an obligation to turn it over to the defense counsel independent of any discovery request.

> *Federal statutes do require that before certain private information is subpoenaed from third parties, the person who the information pertains to should be notified before so that he may file a motion to quash the subpoena. This applies to all proceedings, military and civilian. One instance in which this occurs if when an individual's financial records are subpoenaed from a bank that he has accounts in.

If the party receiving the subpoena objects to it, he may request that the court excuse him from complying with the subpoena by filing a motion to quash the subpoena. Common legal grounds for granting a motion to quash is that the information requested is privileged (such as attorney-client privilege) or that it is an undue burden to produce the evidence (for instance, if a corporation was requested to release thousands of pages of records scattered over several different locations). If the military judge grants the motion to quash, the person or entity receiving the subpoena is exempt from complying with it. If the military judge denies the motion to quash and the subpoena is still not complied with, then the military can seek to have the noncompliant person criminally punished in civilian federal court. The military judge's ruling on a motion to quash a subpoena may be appealed to the appropriate military appellate court.

Motions to quash are rare in the military; however, recently there has been substantial litigation dealing with motions to quash. In a few high-profile war crimes cases, the accused spoke with the media regarding the charges. The military has sought to subpoena the reporters' notes from those interviews, and the reporters have been in ongoing litigation with the military over whether those notes are privileged.

Unlike the trial counsel, however, if the defense counsel wishes to subpoena evidence, he must request the trial counsel to issue the subpoena for him. If the trial counsel refuses, then the defense can request the court to order the subpoena issued. This can be a serious tactical disadvantage to the defense since they are required beforehand to tell the trial counsel what they are looking for. This gives the trial counsel advance notice as to what evidence the defense is looking for and where the defense believes that it might be found. From that the trial counsel can potentially glean what the defense's theme and theory of the case will be before the defense counsel announces it in his opening statement.

There is no reason that at the very least the military defense counsel should be given the same subpoena authority that the trial counsel has. The ability to independently subpoena evidence is not a huge advantage, but it can affect the outcome of certain cases. The military defense counsel should have the same authority and be on equal standing with the trial counsel. This is an easy step that would help make the military justice system fairer. Again, this is in keeping with many civilian justice systems in which counsel for both sides have the authority to issue subpoenas. Service members deserve no less than their civilian counterparts.

Inexperienced and Incompetent Judge Advocates

Perhaps the most serious source of injustice arising from the counsel comes from the lack of experience and skill of many judge advocates in the area of criminal law. As with any profession in any organization, there are both good and bad judge advocates, and there always will be both good and bad judge advocates. However, the military should be taking the necessary steps to improve the overall quality of its judge advocates.

The biggest reason for poor criminal law practice by judge advocates is lack of experience. Brand-new attorneys with no criminal experience are often assigned complex cases on their own. This can produce disastrous results on both sides. Dangerous criminals are set free to continue to prey on the military and society because junior trial counsel lack the experience and skills to properly prosecute the case. Innocent men are wrongfully convicted because their defense counsel did not know how to properly defend a case. The outcome of courts-martial is very important and should not be trusted to judge advocates who are not ready for the responsibility. Having poor counsel results in bad verdicts at courts-martial, and many of these cases are not reviewable by the appellate courts. Ineffective assistance of counsel claims (where the defense counsel does such a poor job that the court overturns all or part of a case because the accused did not receive a fair trial) require a very high standard to prove. For instance, if the defense counsel makes a poor closing argument it can easily cause someone to be wrongfully convicted, but a poor closing argument will very rarely be considered ineffective assistance of counsel. On the flip side, the government cannot appeal a finding of not guilty, so if a dangerous criminal is set free because the trial counsel does not do a good job, the government has no recourse and there is no way to correct the error.

There are several problems that lead to inexperienced attorneys being assigned cases that they are not yet ready to handle. First is that on most bases, there is nothing that requires a counsel to have a certain level of experience before he takes on a certain case. Judge advocates are generally considered ready to try any case after graduating from their service's justice school. Unfortunately, that simply is not the case. A few extra months in school does not make a brand-new attorney ready to try a difficult case. It takes years of experience actually trying cases to be ready to handle the most challenging of cases. Many senior defense counsel do try to assign cases based on the qualifications of counsel under them, but unfortunately, not all do. And often, there are no judge advocates at a particular base qualified to handle difficult cases.

It is that lack of qualified judge advocates to give the cases to that is the most difficult problem to fix. Several different problems contribute to a lack of qualified judge advocates handling criminal matters.

First, the military, and especially the Marine Corps, does not do enough to retain their better judge advocates. Depending on the year, as many as more than half of the captain (O-3), judge advocates eligible to leave the Marine Corps do in fact leave. And it is often the better judge advocates that leave because they are the ones that are able to get the better civilian positions. Judge advocates leave for a host of reasons, but the single biggest factor is generally the poor military pay. A good attorney can make a lot more as a civilian than as a judge advocate. And unlike in the civilian sector where pay and promotions are usually primarily based on how good one is at his job, in the military they are primarily based on how long an individual has served.

Another problem leading to inexperienced judge advocates is programs that send officers to law school to become judge advocates. Different branches have different names and requirements for these programs, but they all essentially work the same. An officer, generally an O-3, is sent to law school while on active duty. Some of the programs pay the officer's salary and for the schooling; some pay part of one or the other. Either way, the officer is still in the military, and when he graduates from law school, he is generally at least a senior O-3 and often an O-4. Because of their higher rank, these officers are then put in positions of greater responsibility. I have seen officers fresh out of law school, with literally no experience, given important positions like military justice officer or senior defense counsel. Not only are these officers not ready to try important cases that someone in their billet is required to be ready to try, but they also lack the ability to train the judge advocates under them as they themselves are still in need of training. The result is more inexperienced, poorly trained judge advocates across the board. These programs need to be eliminated; they are a major source of military injustices.

Another problem that contributes to a lack of criminal experience is the rapid turnover in the judge advocate community. Judge advocates often change billet, or jobs, every eighteen months. To make matter even worse, in the Marine Corps, judge advocates often spend time working in nonlegal billets. These billets include working in recruiting, boot camp, and with personnel issues at headquarters. The result is many judge advocates become jacks-of-all-trades and masters of none. In a six-year span, it is not unusual for a judge advocate to spend only eighteen months in military justice, either as a trial counsel or as a defense counsel. It is unusual for a judge advocate to spend more than three of those years in military justice billets. Once a judge advocate becomes major (O-4), he is often transitioned out of billets that directly involve military justice. As a result, most judge advocates that are trying cases are inexperienced. Just as they are getting experienced, they are often transferred to a different billet, especially once they become majors. Too much is at stake in criminal cases to allow the fate of service members to rest in the hands of judge advocates who are not experienced in military criminal law. The military needs to ensure that it keeps enough judge advocates in trial billets long enough to ensure that they have a significant number of judge advocates at all times with substantial trial experience.

One last problem that tends to be especially prevalent in the Marine Corps is that judge advocates view themselves as Marines and officers first, and attorneys secondarily. As such, some judge advocates spend a great deal of time focusing on making themselves good Marines and officers and very little time on making themselves good attorneys. Our service members, our services themselves, and even our society deserve to have a quality judge advocate representing their interests in court. Judge advocates need to put more emphasis on being good attorneys and not spend the time that should be spent on sharpening legal skills on sharpening military skills.

Government Control of Defense Counsel

One of the most subtle and dangerous sources of military injustice is mostly unique to the Marine Corps. This injustice occurs when the accused's own military counsel is pressured either directly or indirectly to do less than his best on a case. This pressure comes from the command structure that exists for Marine Corps defense counsel. In a typical setup, all judge advocates, to include defense counsel, are attached to a headquarters-type battalion, often call *headquarters and service battalion*. This battalion will contain the headquarters element and logistical-type units for the base. This battalion is often quite large, and in addition to judge advocates, it includes military police, facilities maintenance, finance, and so on. The commanding officer of this unit is generally a colonel (O-6), and he is the convening authority for the unit. Thus, the commanding officer of the defense counsel is also a convening authority.

The potential for abuse from this type of relationship is great and has already been recognized by the Air Force. In the Air Force, the defense counsel's commanding officer is the regional defense counsel. This keeps a completely separate relationship between convening authorities and defense counsel. Even the Marine Corps recognizes that the command structure that they have created is fraught with conflicts of interest and peril to the impartiality of the legal system. However, instead of completely separating out the defense counsel as the Air Force does, the Marine Corps only partially separates defense counsel from the convening authority.

In the Marine Corps, the regional defense counsel controls the daily routine of the defense counsel and writes his fitness reports, but the defense counsel still belongs to the commanding officer of the headquarters battalion. That means that the commanding officer can reassign the defense counsel.* The commanding officer also controls various administrative matters such as granting leave, assigning collateral duties, and ensuring that training standards and requirements are being met (things such as physical fitness tests, rifle and pistol qualifications, weight standards, swim qualifications, and so on.)

*Typically, most commanding officers do not personally assign judge advocates; they allow their staff judge advocate to do it for them. But still the staff judge advocate is the commanding officer's attorney and works on his behalf.

So although the commanding officer and the staff judge advocate do not directly control the defense counsel, they can make his life difficult. Defense counsel, especially junior ones, are prone to try to placate the commanding officer and the staff judge advocate as much as possible in order to keep their lives easy. Of course, the staff judge advocate and the commanding officer are not permitted to attempt to influence the defense counsel—that is called *unlawful command influence* (UCI)—and can result in a case being dismissed. So whereas cases where the commanding officer or the staff judge advocate attempt to directly influence the defense counsel are rare, indirect coercion from the inherently coercive relationship are not. For instance, when a defense does something in a case that upsets the commanding officer or the staff judge advocate, the staff judge advocate will come down and yell at the defense counsel and tell him how screwed up he is and what a bad Marine he is and how he needs to stop doing what he is doing. I have had this happen to me, and I have seen it happen to other defense counsel. A good defense counsel will ignore this and press on zealously representing his client regardless of how the commanding officer or the staff judge advocate view his actions. But unfortunately, some defense counsel back off and ease up on the government to avoid upsetting the commanding officer and the staff judge advocate because they can make the defense counsel's life miserable by denying leave, ordering extra collateral duties, reassigning him to another billet, and so on. Again if the defense counsel can present evidence that the commanding officer or staff judge advocate is taking action against him because of his action in a case, he can request that the military judge order the case dismissed because of unlawful command influence. However, commanding officers and staff judge advocates that engage in these tactics are clever; they are careful about what they say to a defense counsel in such a way to give them plausible deniability, or they simply claim they never said anything at all and it becomes the defense counsel's word against theirs. The worst situation is when a commanding officer or staff judge advocate reassigns the defense counsel to another job, often one that the defense counsel did not want. They then claim that the defense counsel is doing a poor job in his new billet and give him an adverse fitness report. Not only is the defense counsel left doing a job he did not want to, but he is also now unlikely to be promoted and will be required to leave the Marine Corps. Unfortunately, even if the commanding officer and the staff judge advocate would never take such actions, some defense counsel fear that they might, and so they do not represent their clients as zealously as they should.

These types of situation tend to be at their worse when they involve cases where the defense counsel's commanding officer is the case's convening authority. But since the staff judge advocate actually exercises a great deal of the commanding officer's authority on his behalf when dealing with judge advocates, the potential for abuse exists in any case where the staff judge advocate over the defense counsel is the staff judge advocate to the convening authority of the case. These situations are also not as likely to occur at the largest bases, which have a legal services support section (LSSS). A legal services support section has an officer in charge overseeing it, and he has most of the authority over counsel that the staff judge advocate has at the other bases.

This situation where the defense counsel's commanding officer in a convening authority produces disastrous results and casts a cloud over the entire justice system of the Marine Corps. The Marine Corps needs to use the same command structure that the Air Force uses. This eliminates this coercive environment and allows defense counsel to zealously represent their clients free of fear that there zealous representation might adversely affect them personally. The Marine Corps' stubborn refusal to switch to this proper command structure just further cements that notion that the Marine Corps is taking an unjust advantage in its military justice system to get the results that it desires.

PROCEDURAL INJUSTICES

This section addresses various procedural injustices that exist in the military justice system. The way to correct these various procedural injustices is also to change the military justice system to match the civilian justice system in these areas.

Dual-Sovereign Rule

The Constitution protects individuals from being twice tried for the same offense. This is known as *protection from double jeopardy*. However, the prohibition against double jeopardy is not an absolute bar from being tried twice for the same offense. Double jeopardy only prohibits the same sovereign from twice trying the same offense. This is known as the *dual-sovereign rule*. Thus, the federal government can only try an individual once for the same crime, and a state government can only try an individual once for the same crime, but there is no constitutional prohibition against both the state and the federal government trying an individual for the same offense.* In the civilian justice systems, it is extremely rare to see an individual tried for the same offense by both the state and the federal government. In the military, it is not as rare. A court-martial is a federal court. The official policy is that a service member tried by a state court is only to be also tried by court-martial in special circumstances. In the military, it is not commonplace to have a service member court-martialed for the same crime that he was tried for by a state court, but it does happen. The military justice system should not be allowed to try a service member for the same crime that he is tried for by a state simply because the military believes that the punishment received at the hands of the civilian justice system was too lenient or that the service member was acquitted when he should not have been. It is generally fundamentally unfair to be tried twice for the same offense, hence, the constitutional right to be free from double jeopardy. The military finds too many special circumstances that justify a military trial for an offense that was already tried by a state court. Because of this history of abuses, the power should simply be taken away.

> *There can be multiple trials by the same sovereign for the same offense if the first trial is declared a mistrial or sometimes when the first is overturned on appeal. The earlier trial that was declared a mistrial or that was overturned is considered to have never happened for purposes of double jeopardy since the trial was "undone" for being "defective."

No Bail

Another source of continual injustices is the military's system of pretrial confinement (PTC). In the civilian justice systems, when a person is arrested pending trial, he is usually allowed to post bail and remain free until he is sentenced, if he is found guilty. This is to help ensure that individuals who are eventually acquitted or are not sentenced to jail time do not spend months or even years in jail pending the outcome of their trial. The military does not have bail. If a service member is placed in pretrial confinement, he remains incarcerated until he is released by his commanding officer or by the military legal system, or until his trial is finished.

This is a serious problem that results in some service members spending many long months locked in the brig only to be acquitted at trial or to be given a sentence that is less than the one that they have already served. In order to alleviate the issue of service members, who are constitutionally presumed innocent until they are found guilty, spending long periods of time in confinement prior to trial, the military requires that service members in pretrial confinement receive speedy trials. However, this does not solve the problem as it is not unusual for a service member to be in pretrial confinement for several months and, for complicated cases, as much as six months while awaiting his trial. This is a travesty of justice that those who put their lives on the line for our freedom are not afforded the same right to bail that civilians have.

The system is currently set up so that when a service member is placed in pretrial confinement by his command, the commanding officer has to send a letter to the brig stating the reasons why confinement is necessary. The Uniform Code of Military Justice authorizes confinement when there is probable cause that (1) an offense was committed; (2) the prisoner committed it; (3) that confinement is necessary because it is foreseeable that (a) the prisoner will not appear for his court-martial or (b) that he will engage in serious criminal misconduct; and (4) that less severe forms of restraint (such as restricting the service member to base) are inadequate.

The service member then appears before an IRO (initial reviewing officer) for a hearing commonly referred to as an *IRO hearing*. The initial reviewing officer is a neutral officer, generally an O-5 or O-6, who serves as an initial reviewing officer as a collateral duty. They are not required to be judge advocates, although they can be. The accused is represented by military defense counsel at the initial reviewing officer hearing, but that counsel is only assigned for that hearing and may or may not be the counsel that represents him at his court-martial. The command is represented by a trial counsel and often sends a senior member of the command along as a command representative (spokesman) for the command as well. There are no rules of evidence and frequently no witness at an IRO hearing. The initial reviewing officer will review that documentation provided by the command and all law enforcement reports, if there are any. The accused is also allowed to present evidence although since he usually sees his attorney for the first time an hour or so before the hearing and he has been in confinement, he is rarely able to do so. The initial reviewing officer then makes the determination if the continued pretrial confinement is authorized by the Uniform Code of Military Justice. Unfortunately, the way most initial reviewing officers view the Uniform Code of Military Justice (and hence the reason that they are continually assigned as initial reviewing officers by the general or admiral) is that if a service member is facing charges that could result in years on incarceration, then of course it is foreseeable that he would flee to avoid his court-martial. As a result, most service members that are placed in pretrial confinement for allegations that they committed serious crimes generally stay in pretrial confinement. Once the charges against the accused are referred to a court-martial, the accused may request that the military judge review the pretrial confinement and order him released. I did successfully petition military judges on several cases to release my client from pretrial confinement. However, by the time that the accused is able to bring the matter before a military judge, he will generally have already served two to three months of confinement.

The lack of bail is a serious injustice, and like most injustices in the military system, it can be rectified by adapting the same laws of the civilian justice system. Some service members who are a legitimate danger to others or are a legitimate flight risk should not be released on bail, just the same as bail is denied for some civilians, but like the majority of civilians, the majority of service members should be released on bail while pending their trial.

Inexperienced Investigating Officers

Another common source of injustices arises from appointing inexperienced investigating officers (IOs)* for article 32 hearings. The *Manual for Courts-Martial* does not even require that the investigating officers be a judge advocate. In fact, in the Army, the investigating officer is rarely a judge advocate. Even in other branches of the military where judge advocates are assigned as investigating officers they are often very junior or even brand new attorneys. It is not unusual in the Marine Corps to have the investigating officer be a judge advocate that has never even tried a case. I personally served as an investigating officer before ever trying a case. It is actually unusual to see an experienced investigating officer at many bases unless the case is one that is likely to generate media coverage or the case involves potentially capital charges.

*Also referred to as article 32 officers

This creates injustices for both the government and the defense. The investigating officer is supposed to be an independent investigator that holds a hearing to determine whether there is sufficient evidence to go forward on the charges, whether the charges are in the proper form, and whether there should be additional charges. After making his determination he makes a recommendation to the convening authority on how to proceed with the case.

After the case is referred to a court-martial the government can only make minor changes to the charges without the consent of the accused.* Thus it is very important that the government have the charges in the proper form. For the charges to be in the proper form, they must meet the statutory requirements and they must charge the accused with the proper criminal act at the proper time and in the proper location. However, when the investigating officer does not have experience trying cases it is unlikely that he will catch and correct errors in the charges. Around a quarter of the cases that I handled had one or more charges that were referred to trial after the article 32 hearing with errors. Some of them were just embarrassing minor errors such as typos and some of them where major errors that kept the government form being able to get a conviction on a charge that they otherwise probably would have been able to get a conviction on.

> *Sometimes the accused, for tactical reasons, will consent to a major change. The government is sometimes able to simply dismiss all the charges without prejudice and start all over with the correct charges. So in some cases, if the defense feels it is advantageous to go to trial sooner rather than delay the trial by requiring the government to start the case all over, the defense will agree to the change.)

Also once a case is referred to trial new charges cannot be added to the case without the accused's consent.* Thus it is very important to ensure that all charges are referred at once. To accomplish this, the investigating officer needs to properly examine the evidence to see if all the charges that are supported by the evidence have been charged. He also needs to be able to procure additional evidence if there is evidence that is missing that could be the basis for further charges. Again, if the investigating officer is an inexperienced judge advocate, or even worse not a judge advocate at all, it is unlikely that he will be able to properly do this.

> *Again, sometimes an accused will consent to having the additional charges added to the

existing court-martial if he believes that the
government will go forward with a second
court-martial on the additional charges and
that it would be beneficial for him to have only
one court-martial.

In the end, inexperienced investigating officers and
investigating officers who are not judge advocates,
result in wasted time and money for the government
and can result in criminals unjustly being set free.
But the inexperienced investigating officer also hurt
the defense.

An investigating officer is supposed to be a neutral
and impartial part of the military justice system. Part
of his report is to include evidence that suggests an
accused in not guilty and evidence that is in extenuation
or mitigation of the accused's alleged offenses. Again,
the inexperienced investigating officer will often lack
the skill to properly do this.

Another problem for the defense with inexperienced
investigating officers is that they will often be unwilling
to recommend that a case be dismissed. It is always a lot
easier and generates less pressure for the investigating
officer if he agrees with the government. Investigating
officers need to have the experience and the
temperament that often only comes with experience to
make the difficult decisions, even if they are unpopular.

A major reason that commanding officers appoint
inexperienced investigating officers, or worse ones that
are not even attorneys, is that the investigating officer's
recommendation is just that – a recommendation.
The government is free to completely ignore the

investigating officer's report and recommendation. For example, if the investigating officer recommends that all charges be dropped because there is no evidence to support hem, the convening authority can completely ignore the investigating officer and still charge the accused. And that leads directly to the next injustice.

Nonbinding Article 32 Hearings

Probably the most serious procedural injustice in the military justice system is that the article 32 hearing produces only a recommendation and not a decision that binds the government. The article 32 hearing is commonly referred to as the military equivalent of a civilian preliminary hearing. In fact, it is nothing like a civilian preliminary hearing and it is very misleading to call it the civilian equivalent of a preliminary hearing. A preliminary hearing is held before a judge. At the hearing, the government must produce evidence that proves that it more likely than not that the defendant committed each of the charged crimes. If the government fails to do so the judge will dismiss that charge, or the entire case if there are no charges that the government is able to prove by a preponderance of the evidence that the defendant committed them. On the other hand, at an article 32 hearing the government can produce absolutely no evidence on a specific charge and the investigating officer can recommend that the charge be dismissed because he has not been presented with any evidence to support it and the convening authority can still refer the charge to trial. I have seen this happen several times.

*Not all states use a preliminary hearing. Some states use a grand-jury system where the grand jury determines whether or not charges should go forward against the defendant. A defendant is indicted if the grand jury determined that charges should go forward. Some states allow grand juries to indict anyone, not just cases that the prosecutor brings for an indictment.)

After the article 32 hearing, the staff judge advocate writes a recommendation to the convening authority. In order for a case to be referred to a general court-martial, the staff judge advocate must advise the convening authority that the military has jurisdiction in the case and that the charge is warranted by the evidence. However, in my experience, even in the cases where the investigating officer found no evidence, the staff judge advocate still always stated that the evidence supported the charge. The staff judge advocate is the convening authority's attorney and works for him. The staff judge advocate also does not attend the article 32 hearings. As such, this is an inadequate attempt to make the article 32 hearings more like preliminary hearings, as evidenced by the fact that staff judge advocates routinely find evidence to support a charge when the investigating officer did not.

The article 32 system as it is currently set up allows for abuses and injustices. However, these injustices are very easy to correct. Like most injustices, this one too can be fixed by requiring the military to adapt the approach used by the civilian justice system. The article 32 hearing should be a true preliminary hearing.

It should be conducted before at least a senior judge advocate if not a military judge and the results should be binding on the convening authority. Thus in cases where the government is unable to show by even a preponderance of the evidence that the accused committed the charged crimes, that accused would not have to unjustly stand trial for those crimes.

War Crimes

War crimes are perhaps one of the most sensitive areas and the most difficult to deal with in a just manner. Service members certainly should not be allowed to get away with cold-blooded murder simply because it is committed in a war zone. The problem lies in what may be considered cold-blooded murder if it is committed in a time of peace may be justifiable self-defense when committed in a time of war. There are always some clear-cut cases, for instance, if a service member in a secure location shoots an unarmed detainee in his cell. But what about a case where a service member shoots a child approaching a checkpoint because the child did not stop when ordered to?* Or what about when a service member in the middle of a firefight in a crowded city rounds a corner and sees someone running and shoots them in the back?**

> *(Children have been used as suicide bombers and in some conflicts pre-teen children serve as soldiers.)

> **(Insurgents dress like civilians and that individual could be an insurgent fleeing the

battle or trying to find a more secure location
from which to engage the service member.)

There will always be a lot of close cases and difficult decisions to make when charging war crimes. In no area should the government be more positive that it has proof that a crime was committed before they charge a service member. These are usually young men, often only teenagers, and they are making literally life-and-death choices in a split second with no time to weigh the options. Making the wrong choice cannot only result in their own death but also the death of their comrades as well. That is a tremendous amount of responsibility placed on someone that is often so young we do not even allow them to drink alcohol. And in no situation is there more potential for abuse than in this area. Truly, this area alone requires all the changes spoken of in this book. Service members can be charged with war crimes because it is simply the easy thing to do. Service members can be charged because politicians are calling for it. On the other end of the spectrum, evil people using wartime situations can commit heinous crimes, and the justice system can use the war to cover up the crimes and protect the perpetrators. Currently, America has seen a lot more of the former than the latter, but the danger exists for either to happen.

Our service members who are actually on a daily basis risking their lives at the request of our nation must be afforded a just legal system. How barbaric we are to allow them to be subjected to an unjust criminal system that we as citizens do not subject ourselves to. Indeed, our service members fight to defend our constitution which we use as a shield to protect us from unjust criminal systems. They deserve no less protection than us, especially while they are fighting and dying for our nation.

CONCLUSION

We are privileged to live in America. Much of the world is governed by justice systems far worse than our military justice system. But one of the most poignant things about being an American is our power to change our government. In the area of justice for the men and women that serve our country, we need to change. If the changes in this book are implemented, justice still will not be done in every case, but many injustices will be eliminated. Although not perfect, our civilian justice system is a good system. Our service members deserve those same protections. They bear enough burdens without worrying about whether justice will be done should they ever find themselves accused of a crime.

While I will always hold the Marine Corps in high regard and will value my years of service, I cannot allow the need for change to go unnoticed. I cannot allow an unjust system to let criminals escape justice. I cannot allow my Marine brethren to be placed in harm's way and then betrayed by a system they pledged their hearts and lives to defend. Someone must protect those who sacrificially protect us. That protection must begin with the military justice system, but that justice system is fatally flawed and must be changed.

EPILOGUE

I have often been asked why I became a criminal defense attorney. If you knew me, you would understand that this position is a far cry from the "fundamentalist prosecutor" most would consider me to be. Many people think all criminal defense attorneys fall into one of three categories: greedy persons who sell their soul in the name of profit, antigovernment and immoral hippies, or bleeding-heart liberals.

I can assure you that I am none of the above. I am a Christian and a conservative. I believe that the love of money is wrong, as Christ taught. If my life's aim were money, I certainly would not have served in the Marine Corps. I am not antigovernment. I tend to be as pro–law and order in my political beliefs as any person can get. I certainly am not a bleeding-heart liberal. I am politically conservative, and I am not an emotionally driven idealist. Though I am a sinner like all mankind; I strive through the power of my Lord to live my life in a Christ-pleasing, moral way.

So why am I a criminal defense attorney? Originally, I was one because the Marine Corps assigned me to that position. I preferred working as a trial counsel. But eventually, I began to enjoy the work and sought to take on as many cases as I could. Upon leaving the Marine Corps, I prayed seriously about my next career steps. God called me to continue as a defense attorney.

Many of my colleagues tell people that they are defense attorneys to protect our justice system. Our system only works if there are zealous advocates for those who are charged, whether the defendant is factually guilty or innocent. And I agree with that. Many of my colleagues say that the system only works if we are holding the government to its burden which in turn protects those who have not been charged. This prevents the government from becoming a police state that abuses the rights of the people. I agree with that as well.

But the reason I am a defense attorney is much deeper than the typical political or philosophical answers. All men are sinners, whether they are criminals or not. All sinners have justly earned an eternity in hell. Yet Christ so loved us in our sins that He died to pay the price for them. If we accept Him and His blood on the cross as the payment for our sins, we can have heaven as our eternal home. The Bible teaches that Satan accuses each of us before God, the ultimate judge. Satan's accusations are true as we have all sinned. Yet we have available to us (at no charge if we chose to accept Him) the greatest defense attorney ever—Jesus Christ. Scripture teaches us that He is our advocate (defense attorney) before God, the judge. And He never loses a case. He pleads that Satan is correct, that justice demands punishment for our sins, but that He has already paid that price on our behalf.

So if Christ is my advocate, even though I am guilty and worthy of hell, how can I refuse to be an advocate for my fellow man, whether he is guilty or not? I hope to show the love of God through my work to the most unloved in our society and thus to bring honor and glory to Him. That is my calling in this profession.